THE RENAISSANCE

Studies in European History

General Editor: Richard Overy
Editorial Consultants: John Breuilly
                         Roy Porter

PUBLISHED TITLES

FORTHCOMING

THE RENAISSANCE

Second Edition

PETER BURKE

Professor of Cultural History
University of Cambridge

Published in Great Britain by
MACMILLAN PRESS LTD
Houndmills, Basingstoke, Hampshire RG21 6XS and London
Companies and representatives throughout the world

A catalogue record for this book is available from the British Library.

ISBN 0–333–66927–4

Published in the United States of America by
ST. MARTIN'S PRESS, INC.,
Scholarly and Reference Division,
175 Fifth Avenue, New York, N.Y. 10010

ISBN 0–312–17230–3

Library of Congress Cataloging-in-Publication Data
Burke, Peter.
The Renaissance / Peter Burke. — 2nd ed.
p.   cm. — (Studies in European history)
Includes bibliographical references and index.
ISBN 0–312–17230–3 (pbk.)
1. Renaissance.   I. Title.   II. Series: Studies in European
history (New York, N.Y.)
CB361.B8   1997
940.2'1—dc20

96–43456
CIP

This book is printed on paper suitable for recycling and made from fully managed and sustained forest sources.

10   9   8   7   6   5   4   3   2   1
06   05   04   03   02   01   00   99   98   97

Printed in Hong Kong

Contents

List of Plates

Editor's Preface

The main purpose of this new series of Macmillan studies is to make available to teacher and student alike developments in a field of history that has become increasingly specialised with the sheer volume of new research and literature now produced. These studies are designed to present the 'state of the debate' on important themes and episodes in European history since the sixteenth century, presented in a clear and critical way by someone who is closely concerned himself with the debate in question.

The studies are not intended to be read as extended bibliographical essays, though each will contain a detailed guide to further reading which will lead students and the general reader quickly to key publications. Each book carries its own interpretation and conclusions, while locating the discussion firmly in the centre of the current issues as historians see them. It is intended that the series will introduce students to historical approaches which are in some cases very new and which, in the normal course of things, would take many years to filter down into textbooks and school histories. I hope it will demonstrate some of the excitement historians, like scientists, feel as they work away in the vanguard of their subject.

The format of the series conforms closely with that of the companion series of studies in economic and social history, which has already established a major reputation since its inception in 1968. Both series have an important contribution to make in publicising what it is that historians are doing and in making history more open and accessible. It is vital for history to communicate if it is to survive.

R. J. OVERY

1 The Myth of the Renaissance

'At the sound of the word "Renaissance"', wrote the Dutch historian Johan Huizinga, 'the dreamer of past beauty sees purple and gold' [11]. More exactly, he or she sees in the minds eye Botticelli's *Birth of Venus*, Michelangelos *David*, Leonardos *Mona Lisa*, Erasmus, the châteaux of the Loire, and the *Faerie Queene*, all rolled into one, into a composite picture of a golden age of creativity and culture.

This image of the Renaissance – with a capital R – goes back to the middle of the nineteenth century, to the French historian Jules Michelet (who loved it), the critic John Ruskin and the architect A. W. Pugin (who disapproved), the poet Robert Browning and the novelist George Eliot (who were more ambivalent), and above all to the Swiss scholar Jacob Burckhardt [15]. It was Burckhardt whose famous *Civilisation of the Renaissance in Italy* (1860) defined the period in terms of two concepts, 'individualism' and 'modernity'. 'In the Middle Ages', according to Burckhardt, 'human consciousness...lay dreaming or half awake beneath a common veil.... Man was conscious of himself only as a member of a race, people, party, family, or corporation – only through some general category.' In Renaissance Italy, however, 'this veil first melted into air...man became a spiritual individual, and recognised himself as such' [1: part 2]. Renaissance meant modernity. The Italian was, Burckhardt wrote, 'the firstborn among the sons of modern Europe'. The fourteenth-century poet Francesco Petrarca (known in English as 'Petrarch') was 'one of the first truly modern men.' The great renewal of art and ideas began in Italy, and at a later stage the new attitudes and the new artistic forms spread to the rest of Europe.

This idea of the Renaissance is a myth. 'Myth' is, of course, an ambiguous term and it is deliberately used here in two different senses. When professional historians refer to 'myths', they usually

1

mean statements about the past which they can show to be false, or at any rate misleading. In the case of Burckhardt's account of the Renaissance, they object to the dramatic contrasts which he makes between Renaissance and Middle Ages and between Italy and the rest of Europe. They consider these contrasts to be exaggerated, ignoring as they do the many innovations which were made in the Middle Ages; the survival of traditional attitudes into the sixteenth century, or even later; and Italian interest in the painting and music of other countries, especially the Netherlands.

The second sense of the term 'myth' is a more literary one [14]. A myth is a symbolic story told about characters who are larger (or blacker, or whiter) than life; a story with a moral, and in particular a story about the past which is told in order to explain or justify some present state of affairs. Burckhardt's Renaissance is a myth in this sense too. The characters in his story, whether they are heroes like Alberti and Michelangelo or villains like the Borgias, are all larger than life. The story itself both explains and justifies the modern world. It is a symbolic story in the sense that it describes cultural change in terms of the metaphors of awakening and rebirth. These metaphors are not merely decorative. They are essential to Burckhardt's interpretation.

The metaphors were not new in Burckhardt's day. From the middle of the fourteenth century onwards, a growing number of scholars, writers and artists in Italy and elsewhere came to use the imagery of renewal to mark their sense of living in a new age, an age of regeneration, renovation, restoration, recall, rebirth, reawakening, or re-emergence into light after what they were the first to call the 'dark ages' [12: ch. 1].

The metaphors were not new in their day either. The Roman poet Virgil paints a vivid picture of the return of the golden age in his Fourth Eclogue, while the idea of rebirth is clearly expressed in the Gospel of St John: 'Unless a man be born again of water and the Holy Ghost, he cannot enter into the Kingdom of God.' If anything was distinctive about the use of these metaphors in the period 1300–1600, with which we are concerned, it was their application to a scholarly or artistic movement, rather than to a political or religious one. In the 1430s, for example, Leonardo Bruni described Petrarch as the first 'who possessed such grace and genius that he could recognise and recall to the light the ancient elegance of style, which had been lost and extinguished'. Erasmus told pope Leo X that 'our age... bids fair to be an age of gold', thanks to the revival of learning as well as piety, while Giorgio Vasari organised his *Lives* of painters, sculptors and architects around the idea of a renewal of the arts in three stages from the beginnings in the age of Giotto to the culminating points of Leonardo, Raphael and, above all, Vasari's own master Michelangelo [20].

Like all self-images, that of the scholars and artists of the Renaissance was both revealing and misleading. Like other sons rebelling against their fathers' generation, these men owed more than they knew to the 'Middle Ages' they so frequently denounced. If they overestimated their distance from the recent past, they underestimated their distance from the remote past, the antiquity they admired so much. Their account of their rebirth was a myth in the sense that it presented a misleading account of the past; that it was a dream, a wish-fulfilment; and that it was a re-enactment or representation of the ancient myth of the eternal return.

Burckhardt's mistake was to accept the scholars and artists of the period at their own valuation, to take this story of rebirth at its face value and to elaborate it into a book. To the old formulae of the restoration or renewal of the arts and the revival of classical antiquity, he added new ones such as individualism, realism, and modernity. The adage 'Before you study history, study the historian' is certainly good advice in Burckhardt's case. There were personal reasons for his attraction to the period and also to this image of it. Burckhardt saw Italy, past and present, as an escape from his native Switzerland, a country he found dull and stuffy. In his youth he expressed his identification with Italy by signing his name as 'Giacomo Burcardo'. He described himself as 'a good private individual', as well as characterising the Renaissance as an age of individualism. These personal reasons do not of course explain the success of the new definition, or the growing interest in the Renaissance in the later nineteenth century (among intellectuals such as Walter Pater, Robert Browning and John Addington Symonds in England and their equivalents abroad). To account for this success we need to evoke the quasi-religious cult of the arts in newlybuilt temples called 'museums', and also the concern with 'realism' and 'individualism' on the part of nineteenth-century artists and writers. Like Erasmus and

Vasari, they projected their ideals onto the past, creating their own myth of a golden age, a cultural miracle.

This nineteenth-century myth of the Renaissance is still taken seriously by many people. Television companies and organisers of package tours still make money out of it. However, professional historians have become dissatisfied with this version of the Renaissance, even if they continue to admire Michelangelo (say), and to find both the period and the movement extremely attractive. The point is that the grand edifice erected by Burckhardt and his contemporaries has not stood the test of time. More exactly, it has been undermined by the researches of the medievalists in particular [12: ch. xi]. Their arguments depend on innumerable points of detail, but they are of two main kinds.

In the first place, there are arguments to the effect that so-called 'Renaissance men' were really rather medieval. They were more traditional in their behaviour, assumptions and ideals than we tend to think – and also more traditional than they saw themselves. Hindsight suggests that even Petrarch, 'one of the first truly modern men' according to Burckhardt, and a figure who will recur in these pages because of his creativity as a poet and a scholar alike, shared many attitudes with the centuries he described as 'dark' [115]. Two of the most famous books written in sixteenth-century Italy, the *Courtier* and the *Prince*, have turned out to be closer to the Middle Ages than they appear. Castiglione's *Courtier* draws on medieval traditions of courtly behaviour and courtly love as well as on classical texts like Plato's *Symposium* and Cicero's *On Duties* [86: ch. 1; 123]. Even Machiavelli's *Prince*, which deliberately turns the conventional wisdom on its head on occasion, belongs in a sense to a medieval genre, that of the so-called 'mirrors' or books of advice to rulers [48, 111].

In the second place, the medievalists have accumulated arguments to the effect that the Renaissance was not such a singular event as Burckhardt and his contemporaries once thought and that the term should really be used in the plural. There were various 'renascences' in the Middle Ages, notably in the twelfth century and to a lesser extent in the age of Charlemagne. In both cases there was a combination of literary and artistic achievements with a revival of interest in classical learning, and in both cases some contemporaries described their age as one of restoration, rebirth or renewal [4, 121].

Some bold spirits, notably Arnold Toynbee in his *A Study of History*, have gone further still in this direction and discovered renascences outside western Europe, whether in Byzantium, the world of Islam, or even in the Far East. 'In using the word renaissance as a proper name', wrote Toynbee, 'we have been allowing ourselves to fall into the error of seeing a unique occurrence in an event which in reality was no more than one particular instance of a recurrent historical phenomenon' [129]. His phrase 'no more than' reduces a complex movement to one of its traits, the revival of antiquity, and runs the risk of attributing equal significance to a number of movements of greater or less originality and importance in their respective cultures. However, Toynbee is surely right to try to locate the Renaissance in world history, and to draw attention not only to the revivals of 'Hellenism' (as he calls the classical tradition) outside western Europe but also to revivals of 'dead' indigenous traditions in China and Japan. Each revival had its specific features, just like an individual person; but all the revivals are in a sense members of the same family.

Toynbee's work raises another question which has become more and more urgent since his day. We are living in an age of widespread discomfort with, if not rejection of, the so-called 'Grand Narrative' of the development of western culture − the Greeks, the Romans, the Renaissance, the Discoveries, the Scientific Revolution, the Enlightenment, and so on − a narrative which can be used to legitimate claims to superiority on the part of western elites. Educated westerners as well as third world intellectuals are less and less at ease with the idea of a single 'great tradition' with a monopoly of cultural legitimacy, or the idea of world history as a drama with a single plot [132].

Where does this leave us? Was there a Renaissance at all? If we describe the 'Renaissance' in purple and gold, as an isolated cultural miracle, or as the sudden emergence of modernity, my own answer would be 'no'. Renaissance architects produced masterpieces, but so did Gothic master masons. Sixteenth-century Italy had its Raphael, but eighteenth-century Japan had its Hokusai. Machiavelli was a powerful and original thinker, but so was the historian Ibn Khaldun, who lived in North Africa in the fourteenth century.

If, however, the term 'Renaissance' is used − without prejudice to the achievements of the Middle Ages, or those of the world

5

beyond Europe – to refer to an important cluster of changes in western culture, then it may be regarded as an organising concept which still has its uses. To describe and interpret this cluster of changes is the task of the remainder of this essay.

2 Italy: Revival and Innovation

Despite the need to revise the accepted account of the Renaissance, which presents the Italians as active and creative and other Europeans as passive and imitative, it is impossible not to start with Italy. This section is therefore concerned with the principal changes in the arts, literature and ideas from Giotto (d. 1337) to Tintoretto (1518–94), and from Petrarch (1304–74) to Tasso (1544–95). It will attempt to replace these changes – whether revivals or innovations – in their cultural and social contexts. It is obvious enough that there was no lack of creative individuals in this period, men – they were indeed males for the most part – who impressed their personalities on their works. All the same, if we look at the course of cultural change in Italy over the long term, over the three hundred years 1300–1600, it becomes equally obvious that the achievements are collective in the sense that small groups worked together and that each generation built on the work of its predecessors. In a relatively brief essay it seems best to stress the collective and to try to see the Renaissance movement as a whole.

What is especially distinctive about this movement is the whole-hearted attempt to revive another culture, to imitate antiquity in so many different fields and media. This is not the only important feature of the Italian Renaissance, but it may not be a bad place to begin.

The revival of classical forms is most obvious in architecture, from the ground-plans to the ornamental details [35, 36, 37]. It is no surprise that this revival should have taken place in Italy, where a number of classical buildings had survived more or less intact, including the Pantheon (Plate 5), the Colosseum, the Arch of Constantine and the Theatre of Marcellus (all in Rome itself), while the climate made the imitation of these buildings more practical in the south of Europe than it could be elsewhere. Generations of architects, including Filippo Brunelleschi (1377–1446), Donato Bramante (*c*.1444–1514), and Andrea Palladio (1508–80), went to Rome to study and measure these buildings in order to follow the principles on which they were built. Their studies were assisted by the survival of a treatise on architecture written by an ancient Roman, Vitruvius. His *Ten Books of Architecture* was first published in 1486 or thereabouts. Vitruvius emphasised the need for symmetry and proportion in architecture, comparing the structure of a building to that of the human body. He also explained the rules for the correct employment of the 'three orders', in other words the Doric, Ionic and Corinthian columns with their appropriate friezes, cornices and so on. The classical system of proportions was followed in such buildings as Brunelleschi's churches of San Lorenzo and Santo Spirito in Florence, and Leon Battista Alberti's San Francesco at Rimini. Bramante's San Pietro in Montorio in Rome (Plate 2), built in 1502 broke with the traditional medieval cruciform church plan to follow the circular plan of a typical Roman temple; hence its Italian nickname of the 'little temple' (*Tempietto*). It was also the first church to utilise the full Doric order. Also reminiscent of a Roman temple is the grand portico of Palladio's Villa Foscari, nicknamed 'the discontented woman' (*La Malcontenta*), built at Fusina near Venice a little before 1560. In this case the order utilised is the Ionic. Roman country houses or villas had not survived, so Renaissance villas, from Poggio a Caiano in the 1480s to Pratolino in the 1570s (both built for the Medici family), drew on the descriptions of his country houses and gardens in the letters of the ancient Roman writer Pliny the younger [38].

In the case of sculpture, there was no ancient treatise like that of Vitruvius, but classical models were of enormous importance all the same [33, 34]. The sculptor Donatello went to Rome, like his friend Brunelleschi, in order to study the remains of classical antiquity, while Buonaccolsi (nicknamed *Antico*), who became famous for his small bronzes, was sent to Rome by his patron, the marquis of Mantua, for the same reason. By 1500 it had become fashionable for Italians of taste to collect classical marbles, and one of the greatest enthusiasts was pope Julius II. Julius owned most of the masterpieces which had been unearthed in his time, including the Belvedere Apollo (named after the papal villa in which it was displayed), and the still more famous Laocoön, which illustrates a scene from Homer's *Iliad* in which a Trojan priest is crushed by serpents sent by Apollo. The new genres of Renaissance sculpture were generally classical genres revived, such as the portrait bust, the equestrian monument, and the figure or group illustrating ancient mythology, such as the young Michelangelo's *Bacchus* (Plate 4), which imitated the classical style with such success that it was believed for a time to be a genuine antique.

In the case of painting, ancient sources and models were much harder to find. There was no equivalent of Vitruvius or even the Laocoön. Apart from a few decorations in Nero's Golden House at Rome, classical painting was unknown at this time, and would remain so until the excavation of Pompeii in the late eighteenth century. Like their colleagues in architecture and sculpture, painters wished (or were encouraged by their patrons) to imitate the ancients, but they had to use more indirect means, posing figures in the positions of famous classical sculptures, or attempting to reconstruct lost classical paintings from descriptions in literary texts [24, 25]. Botticelli's *Calumny* (Plate 3), for example, follows the description of a lost work by the painter Apelles given by the Greek writer Lucian. There was also an attempt to derive rules for painters from the literary criticism of the ancients, on the principle that, as Horace put it, 'as is painting, so is poetry'. Music was another art in which attempts were made – especially in the 1540s and 1550s – to recreate the ancient style on the basis of literary sources, in this case classical treatises [87].

The rise of the portrait as an independent genre was one of the trends which was encouraged by the example of antiquity. Fifteenth-century portraits were usually painted in profile as if imitating the heads of emperors on Roman coins, and they were usually cut short below the shoulders as if they were equivalents of ancient marble busts. It was only around the year 1500 that Leonardo, Raphael and other artists emancipated themselves from this convention, to produce works without classical precedent which showed the sitter in full- or three-quarter-face, half- or full-length, sitting or standing, conversing with friends or giving orders to servants [31].

In painting, however, there was at least one crucial development of the period which took place without reference to antiquity: the discovery of the rules of linear perspective. It is possible that ancient artists had known these rules, but they were lost until their rediscovery by Brunelleschi and his friends in the fifteenth century, an example which illustrates the affinity between the two ages and suggests that the similarities between them cannot be explained in terms of imitation alone.

In both classical and Renaissance times, artists were particularly concerned with the appearance of things, with what Burckhardt called 'realism'. The word is left in inverted commas not only because it has more than one meaning (illusionistic style; subject-matter taken from 'real life', whatever that is, and so on), but also because all artists represent what is real to them and because there can be no art without conventions. Even perspective can be regarded, in the words of the art historian Erwin Panofsky, as a 'symbolic form'. In other words, representing the world according to certain rules meant accepting certain values and rejecting others [29].

In the case of medieval artists, these values have to be inferred from their work, with the consequent danger of a circular argument. Even in the case of Giotto, his concern with three-dimensionality, more especially the solidity of the human figure, has to be inferred in this way. In Italy in the fifteenth and sixteenth centuries, however, artists and others not infrequently expressed their ideas about art in writing and even, at the end of the period, in print, in Vasari's *Lives* and elsewhere. They make very clear what problems they were attempting to solve in their art and also their appreciation of such qualities as 'truth' to nature, the illusion of life, the apparently effortless overcoming of difficulties, and, hardest of all to define, 'grace' [6: ch. 6; 20].

Architecture, sculpture and painting have been discussed first because it is of the visual arts that most of us now think first when we hear the word 'Renaissance'. In the period itself, however, literature and learning, the so-called 'liberal arts', were taken more seriously (at least by the learned) than the 'mechanical arts', a category in which painting, sculpture and architecture were lumped together with agriculture, weaving and navigation, despite the protests of Leonardo and others. The social status of the painter was little different from that of a carpenter, mason or weaver, especially at the beginning of the period. It was only gradually that the new profession of the 'artist' emerged [28, 30].

The metaphor of rebirth was usually applied not to the arts but to *bonae litterae*, 'good letters', in other words language, literature and learning. This was at any rate the opinion of the scholars and writers whose accounts of the great revival have come down to us, since artists (with the distinguished exception of Vasari) left few records of their views on the subject. It is important to keep in mind this bias in the surviving evidence. The main language which was 'reborn' or 'revived' at this time was not Italian, but classical Latin. Medieval Latin was coming to be regarded as 'barbarous', in its vocabulary, its spelling (*michi* in place of the classical *mihi*), its syntax, and so on. 'Not only has no one spoken Latin correctly for many centuries', wrote the scholar Lorenzo Valla in the 1440s, 'but no one has even understood it properly when reading it.' In his day, however, it became the ambition of some scholars to write Latin like Cicero.

These scholars also revived the principal literary genres of ancient Rome: the epic, the comedy, the ode, the pastoral, and so on [74]. As early as the mid-fourteenth century, Petrarch produced a Latin epic, the *Africa*, based on the life of the great Roman general Scipio Africanus. It was the first of many imitations of Virgil's *Aeneid*, in which heroic deeds were narrated according to a set of conventions which included beginning in the middle (with later flash-backs), and alternating deeds done on earth with debates in councils of the gods. Tasso's *Jerusalem Delivered* (1581), a story of the First Crusade, is at once one of the most deeply christian and profoundly classical of Renaissance epics.

In similar fashion, Italian tragedies were written in the melodramatic manner of Seneca, piling the stage with corpses, and comedies in the style of the ancient Roman playwrights Plautus and Terence, complete with heavy fathers, cunning servants, boastful soldiers and mistaken identities. Poetry in Latin and Italian included odes in the manner of Horace, epigrams in the manner of Martial, and pastorals in the manner of Virgil's *Eclogues*, in which shepherds play their pipes in an Arcadian landscape and sing of their yearning for their loves. Ideas were frequently presented in the form not of treatises but of dialogues, inspired by those of ancient writers, notably Plato, Cicero and Lucian. Histories of Florence, Venice and other Italian states were modelled on Livy's history of Rome, while biographies (including Vasari's lives of artists) followed the paradigm of Plutarch's lives of famous Greeks and Romans.

The fact that vernacular literature was taken less seriously than Latin – before 1500, at least – deserves emphasis. Although

11

Petrarch is most appreciated today for his Italian love-lyrics, he would probably have preferred to have been remembered for his *Africa*. Paradoxically enough, it was a dead language, classical Latin, which was the language of innovation. There was a time-lag of more than a century between the first Renaissance come-dies in Latin and their equivalents in Italian such as Ludovico Ariosto's *Suppositi* (1509), and Bernardo Bibbiena's *Calandria* (1513). Leonardo Bruni's Latin *History of the Florentine People* goes back to the early fifteenth century, while the first Italian work in the same class, Francesco Guicciardini's *History of Italy*, was written more than a hundred years later [43, 48]. When contemporaries mentioned the revival of 'letters', they were generally referring not so much to literature in the modern sense as to what is known today as the rise of humanism.

'Humanism' is a somewhat elastic term, with different mean-ings for different people. The word *Humanismus* came into use in Germany in the early nineteenth century to refer to the tradi-tional type of classical education, the value of which was begin-ning to be questioned, while Matthew Arnold seems to have been the first to use the term 'humanism' in English. As for 'hu-manist', the word originated in the fifteenth century as student slang for a university teacher of the 'humanities', the *studia huma-nitatis*. This was an ancient Roman phrase to describe an aca-demic package of five subjects in particular: grammar, rhetoric, poetry, ethics and history [5].

The reader may well be wondering what was particularly human about the humanities, defined in this way. They are so called, wrote Leonardo Bruni, one of the leaders of the move-ment to revive these studies, because they 'perfect man'. But why should these five subjects be regarded as perfecting man? The fundamental idea was that men (in other words humans, gener-ally viewed by male humanists in male terms) are distinguished from animals primarily by the ability to speak and therefore to distinguish right from wrong. Hence the fundamental subjects of study were those dealing with language (grammar and rhetoric) or with ethics. Both history and poetry were regarded as kinds of applied ethics, teaching students to follow good examples and avoid evil ones [46]. The scholars of the period were not afraid to generalise about the 'human condition' (as the Florentine hu-manist Poggio Bracciolini called it), or to compose orations, like the young aristocrat Giovanni Pico della Mirandola, on the 'Dignity of Man' – though this text was not intended by Pico to be a declaration of independence from God [116].

Nor was it intended to be a declaration of the subordination of women. The question of the 'dignity and excellence' of women was often debated in Renaissance Italy, especially in court circles, and women found some distinguished defenders. In Petrarch's time his friend Giovanni Boccaccio compiled the biographies of a hundred and six famous women, from Eve to Queen Joanna of Naples. Castiglione defended the excellence of women in a separate treatise before including a debate on the subject in his famous *Courtier*. At the end of the sixteenth century, two Italian women produced books in defence of their sex, Modesta Pozzo's *The Merit of Women* (1587), and Lucrezia Marinelli's *Nobility and Excellence of Women* (1600). In a certain sense of the term, 'feminism' goes back to the Renaissance [95, 98].

The basic assumptions of the humanists are neatly illustrated in a diagram from an early sixteenth-century treatise by the French humanist Charles de Bouelles (Plate 6). According to this diagram (following Aristotle) there are four levels of existence. In ascending order they are: to exist (like a stone), to live (like a plant), to feel (like a horse) and to understand (like a man). There are four corresponding kinds of human being; the sluggard, suffering from 'sloth;' the glutton; the vain person, represented holding a mirror; and the scholar sitting at his lectern. In other words, humanity is perfectible, but only the humanist is truly human.

The diagram also implies that the life of contemplation, or study, is superior to the life of action. There was in fact no consensus on this issue among humanists. Leonardo Bruni, who was active as chancellor of the Florentine republic, argued that a man could fulfil himself only as a citizen (this is why he has been called a 'civic' humanist), while Marsilio Ficino, a Florentine philosopher who accepted the patronage of the Medici, preferred contemplation [42, 43]. Outside Italy, humanists were also divided on this issue. Erasmus protected his liberty to study and write and refused to be tied down by political or academic commitments. Others were torn between the two ideals. Sir Thomas More found the decision whether or not to become a councillor to Henry VIII (and later Lord Chancellor) a difficult one to

13

take. Montaigne retired to the tower of his country house in order to study, but left it again to become Mayor of Bordeaux at a time of civil war [109, 114, 113].

It will be obvious that the studies most emphasised by the humanist movement did not include what we call 'science' (a common term at the time was 'natural philosophy'). However, some leading humanists, Leon Battista Alberti for instance, were interested in mathematics in particular. In any case, the recovery of the texts of ancient Greek and Roman writers on mathematics, medicine, astronomy, astrology and (not least) magic was part of the humanist programme, and the classical texts were virtually indispensable for the future development of these studies. It may therefore be argued that there was a mathematical, a scientific and even a magical 'Renaissance' in this period [50, 51, 91–3]. In the cases of Brunelleschi, Alberti and Leonardo da Vinci, the links between the arts and the Renaissance of mathematics and science are particularly obvious [35, 110].

In what sense was there a 'rise' of humanism in Italy between 1300 and 1600? Just as there were attempts to revive classical art and literature, an effort was made to imitate the educational system of ancient Rome. One of the pioneers of the new kind of education was Vittorino da Feltre, who ran a small boarding-school at Mantua from 1423 to 1446; another was Guarino da Verona [42, 45: ch. 1]. The new system involved teaching the students to speak and write as well as to read classical Latin, and it also meant an emphasis on the humanities, especially rhetoric, at the expense of other subjects, notably logic. Logic had been central to the introductory arts course in medieval universities, but it was attacked by Petrarch and other humanists on the grounds that it was futile, mere quibbling or hair-splitting, and that it required the use of 'barbarous' (in other words, non-classical) technical terms like 'substance', 'accidents', 'quiddity' and so on [53: ch. 7].

In a few schools and in some Italian universities, notably in Florence (from 1396 onwards), and in Padua (from 1463), it was also possible to study ancient Greek. Classical Athens was not yet such an object of admiration as classical Rome, but the Greek language did attract students. The first professors were refugees from the Byzantine Empire, which was falling piece by piece to the Turks long before the capture of Constantinople in 1453.

14

Thanks to these refugees, some Italian scholars acquired the ability to read important Greek texts in the original language. Some of these texts were newly discovered, including many dialogues of Plato and the works of the mysterious 'Hermes Trismegistus' (believed to be an ancient Egyptian sage), which were translated by Ficino, whose admiration for Plato was so intense that he and his followers are often described as 'neoplatonists' [50: chs 1–4; 53: ch. 3].

Other texts now studied in the original Greek, such as the New Testament and the works of Aristotle, had previously been known in Latin translations. However, the humanists discovered serious discrepancies between these translations (sometimes re-translations of Arabic translations from the Greek) and the original texts. It was because he had read Aristotle in the original Greek that the sixteenth-century Italian philosopher Pietro Pomponazzi became convinced that his medieval predecessor St Thomas Aquinas had been wrong to suggest that Aristotle taught the immortality of the soul. This was to call in doubt the whole Thomist synthesis between Christian doctrine and Aristotle. Thus the quest for accurate translations had as an unintended consequence the discovery that the ideas of the much-admired ancients were more remote and more alien than had formerly been assumed [52: ch. 4].

According to the humanists, even classical Latin texts had long been misunderstood, when they had not been lost altogether. The rediscovery of the classics was an exciting event in the lives of scholars such as Petrarch and his follower Coluccio Salutati (who recovered Cicero's letters between them), and Poggio Bracciolini (who found some of Cicero's speeches). However, it turned out that different manuscripts of the same text contained different readings of key words, so that techniques had to be developed for 'textual criticism', in other words the recovery of what the author had originally written before the chain of copyists distorted the message [126: ch. 12; 130].

Classical texts which had been known in the Middle Ages were given new interpretations. Roman law had been studied in Italian universities, notably Bologna, from the eleventh century onwards, but the humanists were the first to interpret these laws by placing them in the context of the culture and society of ancient Rome, which the study of classical literature and inscriptions was making more familiar to them. It was, for example, his knowledge of Roman history, and more especially of the history of the Latin language, which allowed the humanist Lorenzo Valla to demonstrate, in the middle of the fifteenth century, that the so-called 'Donation of Constantine', a document in which the emperor granted central Italy to the pope and his successors, had nothing to do with Constantine but was written several centuries later. According to Valla, the style of the document was so barbarous that it had to be of later date than it claimed to be [66: ch. 1].

There were two apparently contradictory elements in the attitude to antiquity held by the humanists and the artists associated with them. On the one hand, they were much more conscious than their medieval predecessors of the distance between the classical past and the present, and concerned with what they called the corruption of the language and the decline of the arts after the barbarians invaded Italy. On the other hand, they felt personally close to the great Romans. Petrarch wrote letters to Cicero and others, while Machiavelli described himself as conversing with the ancients. Both men believed that antiquity could be revived. Petrarch took a sympathetic interest in the attempted restoration of the Roman Republic, which lasted – within the city walls – from 1347 to 1354. Machiavelli argued passionately in his *Discourses on Livy* that ancient Roman political and military arrangements, such as the citizen militia, could and should be imitated by modern states [115, 111].

To understand the significance of the revival of classical forms in architecture, say, or in the drama, or the enthusiasm for the discovery and editing of ancient manuscripts, we need to view them as portions of a far more ambitious enterprise. It was nothing less than the restoration to life of ancient Rome. What could this mean? It is not always easy to decide whether the humanists were writing literally or metaphorically, or exactly how much of the past they wanted to bring back. However, the basic idea of revival was much more than a figure of speech. Like the ancients, many humanists believed in a cyclical interpretation of history, according to which one age could be a kind of recurrence or rerun of an earlier one. Some of them thought that they and their fellow-citizens could become 'new Romans', in the sense of speaking like the Romans, writing like them, thinking like them, and

16

emulating their achievements, from the Colosseum and the *Aeneid* to the Roman Empire itself. This idea of a return to the past may have been a myth (as was suggested above). All the same, it was a myth which some people not only believed but lived.

One of the key concepts of the humanists was that of 'imitation'; not so much the imitation of nature as that of great writers and artists. Today, this idea has come to sound strange. We have become accustomed to the idea that poems and paintings are expressions of the thoughts and feelings of creative individuals, and although we are aware that some artists do in fact imitate others, we are inclined to think of this as a sign of their lack of talent or an error on the part of people who have yet to 'find themselves' and develop their personal style. 'Imitation' has become a pejorative term. Writers and artists are anxious to emphasise their originality, spontaneity and independence, and to deny the 'influence' of their predecessors (let alone plagiarism, which has come to be regarded as the theft of someone else's intellectual property). In the Renaissance, on the other hand, although charges of plagiarism were beginning to be made, writers and artists tended to suffer from exactly the opposite anxiety. Although we tend to think of this period as an age of innovation and originality, the artists and writers themselves stressed their imitation of the best ancient models; the Pantheon, the Laocoön, Cicero, Virgil, Livy and so on [77, 78].

This imitation was not slavish. To use a favourite metaphor of the time, it did not 'ape' the ancients. The aim was rather to assimilate the model, to make it one's own, and even, if possible, to emulate or surpass it. It was generally assumed that the 'moderns' had no hope of equalling the achievements of the ancients, let alone of going beyond them, but this assumption was itself a challenge to which some people responded. Michelangelo was able, as we have seen, to pass off one of his statues as a genuine antique. Alberti wrote a Latin comedy which was mistaken for a classical work. A sixteenth-century humanist, Carlo Sigonio, 'discovered' a lost work of Cicero's, which turned out to be a creation of his own.

How close imitations should keep to their originals was a matter for controversy. The poet-scholar Angelo Poliziano was one of those who emphasised the need to maintain some distance from classical models, however prestigious. 'Those who compose on

17

the basis of imitation alone strike me as parrots or magpies bringing out things they don't understand. Such writers lack strength and life' [78: ch. 8]. The sixteenth-century Venetian critic Pietro Bembo believed in imitating Cicero when writing in Latin, but he was also concerned to make Italian a dignified literary language, with the fourteenth-century Tuscan writers Petrarch and Boccaccio as the best models, the modern 'classics'. Bembo's friend Castiglione discussed the paradoxical aspect of imitation. One character in his *Courtier* declares that if we imitate the ancients we do not imitate them, because the ancients themselves did not imitate anyone, to which another character replies that the ancient Romans imitated the Greeks.

The growing sense of historical distance made imitation problematic. 'Whom did the ancients imitate?' some people were asking. Did imitation become inappropriate as times changed? Whether they liked it or not, Renaissance artists and writers were unable to imitate the ancients in more than a partial manner. For one thing, the products of antiquity had survived only piecemeal. In painting, as we have seen, and also in music, there were no products of antiquity available for imitation. Painters and musicians were forced to be free. However, the lack of specific models in certain genres was a minor problem compared with the fundamental fact that the Italians of the Renaissance lived in a very different world from that of the ancients. Their economic, social and political system was very different from that of ancient Rome, with its senators and slaves, its legionaries and latifundia. In this situation the ideal of restoring ancient Rome to life could never be more than a dream.

In reality, Petrarch, Brunelleschi, Alberti, Valla, Mantegna, Ficino, and other scholars, writers and artists of the fourteenth and fifteenth centuries were in many ways distant from what they felt was close – ancient Rome – and close to what they felt was distant, the 'Middle Ages'. Although they rejected the recent past of what they called 'Gothic' art, 'scholastic' philosophy, and 'barbarous' Latinity, they had been brought up in this late medieval culture and in many ways still belonged to it. Trained as they had been in Gothic script, for example, they found ancient Roman inscriptions difficult to read.

Rejecting the late Middle Ages they knew, the humanists sometimes mistook the early medieval period for the antiquity they so much admired. When, for example, the humanist Poggio devised the handwriting which we call 'Renaissance' or 'Italic', he thought he was following classical exemplars, but these exemplars actually came from the early, pre-Gothic Middle Ages. In similar fashion Brunelleschi took the Baptistery in Florence as a model for his architectural reforms, thinking that it was a classical temple, whereas it has turned out to be an example of the Tuscan Romanesque, probably built in the eighth century [126: ch. 27].

Continuities with the Middle Ages are visible as late as the sixteenth century, even in the work of such exemplary 'Renaissance men' as Lodovico Ariosto and Baldassare Castiglione. Ariosto's most famous work is the narrative poem *Orlando Furioso* (1516). It bears the marks of Ariosto's study of classical epic, but even more obvious is its debt to medieval romance, notably to the Charlemagne cycle (Orlando is none other than the hero Roland). The poem is no ordinary romance of chivalry; it treats the medieval material too ironically for that. But it is no simple imitation of classical epic either. It could only have been written by someone who in a sense belonged to both traditions, and so to neither. Ironic detachment is the only possible stance for someone with a foot in both camps [74: part 2].

Again, Castiglione's well-known *Courtier* (1528), despite its references to ancient precedent, notably to Cicero's treatise on the perfect orator, is concerned to discuss the rules for playing a social role unknown in classical Athens or republican Rome but very well known in the Middle Ages. It may be described as a medieval courtesy-book rewritten under the influence of classical ideals of behaviour, or as a creative adaptation of those ideals to fit a non-classical situation. Like Ariosto's poem, it could only have been written by someone with an intimate knowledge of both traditions, ancient and medieval [86, 106].

One area in which the ambiguities and conflicts inherent in the humanist position became manifest was the writing of history. Leonardo Bruni and Lorenzo Valla were among the historians who wanted to write about the recent Italian past while following the model of Livy's history of Rome, including the model of Livy's language. Yet their subject-matter made this impossible; there was no classical Latin term for Lombardy, for example, or for the political factions of Guelf and Ghibelline, for Muslims, for cannon, and so on, because these institutions, groups and objects had not existed in Roman times [47]. It was not possible to pour all the new material into the classical mould. Giorgio Vasari wrote his *Lives* of painters, sculptors and architects in Italian, thus avoiding these linguistic problems, but his work too reveals a tension between his admiration for recent art and his admiration for antiquity. His borrowings from classical texts such as Plutarch's *Lives*, or Cicero's account of the rise and fall of rhetoric or Pliny's *Natural History* cannot hide the fact that his enterprise had no parallel in classical times, and that the reason it had no parallel was that the ruling class of Greece and Rome had not taken artists as seriously as they were being taken in the age of Michelangelo.

However, the contradictions in the humanist position were most obvious when they discussed religion. With very few possible exceptions they were, after all, Christians, not worshippers of the pagan gods. Petrarch, Alberti, Valla and Ficino were all clerics. Alberti and Valla were both in papal service, while the humanist Aeneas Sylvius Piccolomini became pope Pius II. Petrarch, Valla and Ficino all wrote on theology, while Alberti designed churches and wrote the biography of a saint.

Individual creations of the period may sometimes imitate ancient models very closely, but their social and cultural contexts and functions were very different. Many works of the Renaissance are what have been called cultural 'hybrids', classical in some ways but christian in others [24]. For example, an epic poem might be written in classical Latin on the model of Virgil's *Aeneid*, yet deal with the Nativity (as in the case of a work by Jacopo Sannazzaro), or with the life of Christ. A humanist theologian writing in Latin might refer to churches as 'temples', to the Bible as 'oracles', or to Hell as 'Hades', or give a treatise, as Ficino did, the title *Platonic Theology*. A Renaissance tomb might imitate a classical sarcophagus (complete with winged personifications of Victory), yet combine this with images of Christ or the Virgin Mary [33].

This combination of classical and christian is difficult to interpret, as syncretism often is, because it may have been undertaken for such different reasons. After four hundred years, it is not easy to decide whether Ficino was dressing Platonism up as theology or dressing theology up as Platonism. Nineteenth-century histor-

20

ians, including Burckhardt, tended to present the Italian humanists as essentially 'pagans', who paid no more than lip-service to Christianity. Today, on the other hand, scholars are more likely to argue that it was to paganism that lip-service was paid. The use of classical phrases such as 'oracles' in christian contexts may have meant no more than an attempt to write 'pure' Latin. Or it may have been a kind of learned game, like the painter Andrea Mantegna and his friends calling themselves by Roman titles such as 'consul' when they made an excursion to Lake Garda one day in 1464 to look for classical antiquities.

To note the superficiality of some forms of 'paganising' is not to deny that there was some degree of tension between classical values and christian ones, or that contemporaries were conscious of this, or that it worried them. Similar problems had arisen in early christian times. The Fathers of the Church, Augustine and Jerome for example, belonged to two cultures, the traditional classical culture and the new christian one, and they tried, with more or less difficulty, to harmonise the two, to reconcile Athens with Jerusalem. In the case of Jerome, the internal conflict was so acute that it expressed itself in dramatic form, in his dream of being dragged before the court of Christ and condemned for being 'a Ciceronian, not a Christian'.

The Fathers resolved this conflict by means of a compromise, expressed in picturesque fashion by Augustine in his famous image of the 'spoils of the Egyptians'. When the Israelites went out of Egypt, the Old Testament tells us, they took Egyptian treasure with them. In similar fashion, whatever is valuable in the pagan classics may be appropriated by Christians and put to their own uses. In any case, some early Christians believed that the ancient Greeks had learned true doctrine (the so-called 'ancient theology') from the Jews. 'What else is Plato', wrote Eusebius in the fourth century, 'but Moses speaking Attic Greek?'

This compromise appealed to the humanists, whose problem was of course the opposite one of reconciling traditional christian culture with the rediscovered classics. Many of them were interested in the Fathers of the Church, and some, like Ficino, in the ancient theology [64: chs 1–2]. A few scholars, such as the fifteenth-century Greek refugee Gemistos Pletho, may possibly have abandoned Christianity for the worship of the pagan gods, but most humanists wanted to become ancient Romans without ceasing to be modern Christians. Their desire for harmony led them to interpretations of ancient texts which now seem somewhat far-fetched, such as treating Homer's *Odyssey* and Virgil's *Aeneid* as allegories of the soul's progress through life. However, every age tends to see the past in its own image, and we must not imagine that our own is an exception.

In the case of the visual arts, the meaning of the revival of ancient forms is harder to interpret than in the case of literature, because we usually lack evidence of the artist's intentions, but there are signs of attempts to reconcile antiquity with Christianity and also of the use of early Christian models. The circular plan of Bramante's *Tempietto* (Plate 2), for instance, is reminiscent not only of pagan temples but also of a particular type of early Christian church built to commemorate a martyrdom, and San Pietro in Montorio was indeed built to mark the spot where St Peter was supposed to have been crucified [35: ch. 6]. In the case of Michelangelo, his poems help us interpret his paintings and statues, leaving us in no doubt of his desire to combine classical forms with christian meanings [112].

However thoroughgoing it was supposed to be, the revival of antiquity was not intended as a substitute for Christianity. To admit this is of course to blur the distinction between Renaissance and Middle Ages, since classical forms had been imitated in the 'Romanesque' art which preceded the Gothic (as its modern name implies), while classical poets such as Virgil and Horace had been studied in medieval monasteries and universities [126]. We should not see the Renaissance as a cultural 'revolution' in the sense of a sharp or sudden break with tradition. It is more accurate to think of the movement as a gradual development, in which more and more individuals became more and more dissatisfied with elements of their late medieval culture, and more and more attracted to the classical past.

Why did this happen? This question is the most difficult of all, not because it is hard to imagine possible answers but because it is impossible to nail these answers down with precise evidence. Was the cult of antiquity a means to an end, a way of justifying the break with the recent past? Or were these people interested in the ancient world entirely for its own sake? To be plausible, any explanatory account of this collective attempt to revive ancient Greece and Rome must make sense of three factors; the geography of the movement, its chronology and its sociology. Why should such a movement have arisen in north-central Italy? Why should it have gathered increasing momentum in the fourteenth, fifteenth and sixteenth centuries? And why should it have appealed in particular to urban patricians? Let us take these three questions in order.

It does not look like an accident that the revival of antiquity began in Italy, on the very site of the original achievements, for it was Rome, not Greece, which was the main object of enthusiasm – Virgil rather than Homer, the Pantheon not the Parthenon (only rarely did humanists visit Athens, at that time part of the Ottoman Empire). In a metaphorical sense, the humanists were discovering their ancestors, while some noble families claimed literal descent from ancient Romans (the Cornaro family of Venice from Scipio's family, the Cornelii, for example). The material remains of antiquity – coins, tombs, temples, amphitheatres and so on – were relatively familiar to Italians, including of course Italian artists. Indeed, it is difficult to decide whether the classical inspiration in eighth-, twelfth-, or even fourteenth-century Italian art should be interpreted as survival or revival. When imitations of antiquity became more frequent, more thorough and more self-conscious, we speak of the 'Renaissance', but in Italy, unlike other parts of Europe, the classical tradition had never been remote.

Chronology is more of a problem. If the remains of antiquity had so long been part of the Italian landscape (or, in the case of some classical texts, part of the stock of libraries in Verona and elsewhere), why should they have been taken so seriously only from the time of Petrarch onwards? The obvious answer to this question is that the example of antiquity must have come to seem more relevant to contemporary needs. So what had changed? The most conspicuous change was the rise of the north Italian city-state in the twelfth and thirteenth centuries, in other words the seizure of self-government by the towns [7]. The rise of these towns can be explained in economic terms, by the increasing trade between Europe and the Middle East. It is not difficult to see why the merchant oligarchies should have wished to be independent, and the location of these towns on the borders between the dominions of the pope and the emperor made the achievement of independence a smoother process than it might

23

otherwise have been. The ruling groups of these cities came to see themselves as 'consuls' or 'patricians'; their town councils as the equivalent of the 'Senate'; the cities themselves as so many new Romes. The links between independence and identification with antiquity are particularly clear in the case of Florence at the beginning of the fifteenth century, when the threat from Milan helped make the Florentines and their spokesman, the humanist chancellor Leonardo Bruni, more conscious of who they were and of the values, such as 'liberty', which they were defending [16, 43]. But this dramatic episode is only part of a much longer story of a growing sense of affinity with the Romans, to be found in the towns of northern Italy from the twelfth century, if not before.

Attempting to explain the chronology of the Renaissance has already raised the third question, that of its social basis. It is clear that the Renaissance was a minority movement. It was urban not rural, and the praises of the countryside, in pastoral poetry for example, flowed from the pens of individuals whose main residence was their house in town, not the country villa to which they might retreat during the summer. Within the towns, the revival of antiquity appealed to a minority, or more exactly to three minorities. There were the humanists, who tended to be professional men, teachers or notaries. There were the members of the ruling class, patricians, prelates or princes, who extended their patronage to new forms of art and learning. There were also the artists, who were recruited in the main from the children of urban craftsmen and shopkeepers [6: ch. 3].

To what extent humanists and artists shared the same interests is far from clear. Some paintings, such as Botticelli's *Calumny* (Plate 3) or his *Primavera*, presuppose a knowledge of ancient literature which the artist, who left school at thirteen, is unlikely to have possessed, and it has been suggested that the 'programme' of the latter painting must have come from a humanist adviser such as Ficino or Poliziano, who are likely to have been acquaintances if not friends of Botticelli [25: ch. 3].

On the other hand, it is uncertain whether most humanists understood the passionate interest shown by Brunelleschi, Donatello and other artists in the formal aspects of ancient architecture and sculpture. Alberti, who was a friend of Brunelleschi, Donatello and the painter Masaccio, and wrote plays and dialogues as well as designing buildings, was one of the few men to bridge the gap between these two cultures. Even Leonardo da Vinci, despite the breadth of his interests, remained on one side of the divide [110]. The 'universal man' who could master all skills was a contemporary ideal, but it is difficult to find many people who incarnated it, even in an age in which the pressure to specialise was much less than it is today.

In short, the revival of antiquity did not have the same meaning for every social group. It meant something different in Florence, Rome, Venice and so on. This point becomes particularly obvious if we consider the development of the movement over time. In the fourteenth century, we see an increasing interest in the classical past on the part of a handful of enthusiasts, notably Petrarch, who, far from being 'one of the first truly modern men', belonged to late medieval culture, even if he was coming to reject some of its elements. In the fifteenth century, the movement comes to involve leading members of the ruling class, including popes (notably Nicholas V and Pius II), princes (such as the rulers of Ferrara, Mantua and Urbino) and of course Lorenzo de' Medici, the unofficial ruler of Florence. A few women studied the classics at this time and wrote letters and treatises in Latin, though they sometimes discovered, like Isotta Nogarola of Verona, that male humanists, such as Guarino, refused to treat them on equal terms with men [45: ch. 2].

By the sixteenth century, thanks in part to the more rapid diffusion of ideas facilitated by that new invention, the press – the printing of images as well as the printing of texts – an increasing amount of classical culture was assimilated, and the tiny group of early enthusiasts had turned into a large one, including a considerable number of teachers. Indeed, it was now possible to be introduced to many of these ideas and ideals at school. It was becoming fashionable for nobles to discuss the ideas of Plato (as they are shown doing in Castiglione's *Courtier*), to collect classical statues, to commission portraits of themselves, or to have town houses and country villas built in what was called the 'ancient' style. The poetry of Petrarch and Ariosto was familiar to artisans and shopkeepers as well as to the upper classes.

By this time a considerable number of Italian women were involved in the Renaissance movement. A few were active as artists, from Marietta Tintoretto, who assisted her father, to the noble amateur Sofonisba Anguisciola, who painted portraits of family and friends. Many more wrote poetry in the Petrarchan style, including Vittoria Colonna, Marchioness of Pescara, and the Venetian courtesan Veronica Franco. Other ladies were active as patrons, notably Isabella d'Este, Marchioness of Mantua, an enthusiastic art collector who acquired works by such masters as Giovanni Bellini, Perugino, Leonardo and Titian [94, 97].

This enlargement in the public for the Renaissance was not the only significant development in the fifteenth and sixteenth centuries. There were other changes too. The best-known account of the different phases of the movement is the one given by the artist-historian Giorgio Vasari, who distinguished three periods in the arts: early, middle and what is now known as 'High' Renaissance [20]. Vasari writes as if the achievements of each age surpassed those of the one before, while the goals remained the same. It may be argued, however, that the aims of artists and writers gradually changed during the period. In architecture and literature alike, a concern to create according to ancient principles, interpreted flexibly, congealed into an ideal of following the 'rules' encoded in ancient examples. One might say (exaggerating a little for the sake of clarity) that a movement which had once seemed subversive (to some scholastic philosophers at least) had, by the year 1500 or thereabouts, become part of the establishment. It had been institutionalised, routinised, and incorporated into tradition.

Outside Italy, however, the revival of antiquity was still a novelty in 1500. The movement had not yet lost its power to shock. It is to what was happening outside Italy that we must now turn our attention.

3 The Renaissance Abroad: or the Uses of Italy

It should by now be clear that the imitation of antiquity, the distinctive trait of the Renaissance, was no simple process. It was problematic and it was often viewed at the time as problematic. The same has to be said of the imitation of Italian culture in other countries, as this section will try to show.

It is customary to introduce this topic with an account of the activities of Italians abroad and of foreign visitors to Italy, and there is nothing wrong in that. However, students of the subject have long been dissatisfied with the traditional account of the 'diffusion' or 'reception' of the Renaissance abroad, an account which carries the misleading implication that while the Italians were active, creative and innovatory, the rest of Europe was passive, a mere recipient of 'influence' or, to use another metaphor beloved by historians, a 'borrower', eternally in debt to Italy.

What is wrong with this traditional account? For one thing, the dichotomy between 'Italy' and the rest is misleading, because the relation of the remainder of Italy to Tuscany, and more especially to Florence, was not unlike that of other European countries. The new style in architecture, for example, appeared in Venice only after a certain time-lag, and it had to be modified to suit Venetian tastes before it was accepted. In any case, Italy was not the only site of cultural innovation. It was not in Tuscany but at the papal court, at that time established in Avignon, that Petrarch had some of his most important experiences, made some of his most significant friendships, and wrote some of his most famous poems [115]. Again, it was in the Netherlands that the new technique of oil painting was developed in the early fifteenth century by Jan van Eyck, Roger van de Weyden, and others, and this technique became influential in Italy, where

27

paintings by Flemish masters were much appreciated. In music, the Netherlands was recognised as pre-eminent, even by Italians; the Donatello of music, as one Italian writer put it, was Johannes Ockeghem, and its Michelangelo was Josquin des Près [88]. Major artists and writers such as Albrecht Dürer and Hans Holbein, Erasmus and Montaigne, Shakespeare and Cervantes were all inspired by Italian models, but not by these alone, and in any case they did not follow their models slavishly. In other words, the traditional account of the diffusion or – to use the traditional term – the 'reception' of the Renaissance is misguided. But what can we put in its place?

Historians and literary critics alike have recently been undermining the dichotomy between cultural 'production' and 'consumption', and emphasising the way in which we all modify the cultural 'goods' we acquire and adapt them to our needs. So at this point it may be worth asking what the uses of Italy were for artists, writers and scholars from other parts of Europe in the fifteenth and sixteenth centuries, thus switching attention from what one might call 'supply' to 'demand' and looking not so much at what was borrowed (let alone from whom), as at the process by which it was assimilated, absorbed, reworked, domesticated, transformed. In other words, this version of the 'reception' of the Renaissance outside Italy will attempt to take account of what has come to be known as 'reception theory', the attempt by some students of literature to replace the simple idea of 'influence' by the more subtle one of a process of creative misinterpretation. So when we look at the Italians abroad, we need to ask not only who went where, at what time, and for what purpose, but also what kind of reception – in yet another sense of the term – they received.

Italian humanists and artists seem to have gone abroad in two separate waves [67: ch. 7]. The humanists went first. Although Petrarch had made visits to the Netherlands and to Paris in the fourteenth century, the real humanist brain drain seems to have taken place between the 1430s and the 1520s, with the late fifteenth century as the period in which the intellectual emigration was at its height. Italian scholars went to France, to Hungary, to England, to Spain, to Poland, to Portugal. Few of those who left Italy were in the top flight; indeed, one is entitled to suspect that some of these expatriates migrated because they were not able to find a good position at home. As for the artists, a rather more

28

distinguished group, most of them went abroad about a generation later than the humanists, so that the process was at its height in their case in the early sixteenth century. As in the case of the humanists, the largest cluster of émigrés was to be found in France, among them the painters Rosso and Primaticcio, the goldsmith Benvenuto Cellini, the architect Sebastiano Serlio, and Leonardo da Vinci, all invited by King François I, one of the greatest patrons of the Northern Renaissance [58].

Why did they go abroad? Today, the decision to travel or even to work abroad may be taken relatively lightly, but in those days the difficulties and dangers of travelling as well as the pain of exile must have made the decision a difficult one in most cases. Some artists and humanists left Italy for reasons which had little to do with the Renaissance. A few of them went on diplomatic missions, like Aeneas Sylvius Piccolomini (later pope Pius II) in Central Europe, or Baldassare Castiglione, who ended his life as papal nuncio in Spain. Others were exiles for political or other reasons. Filippo 'Callimaco', for example (nicknamed after an ancient Greek scholar-poet), a man who made an important contribution to the development of humanism in Poland, had had to leave Italy in a hurry after the conspiracy in which he had been involved was unsuccessful.

The religious exiles of the period are well known. Lelio and Fausto Sozzini, for example, were scholars from Siena who found it prudent to leave Italy in the mid-sixteenth century to escape the Inquisition, because they did not believe in the doctrine of the Trinity (it is after them that rejection of this doctrine has come to be known as 'Socinianism'). The Sozzinis and other exiles such as Peter Martyr Vermigli, who found refuge in Oxford, belong to the category of Italian humanists abroad no less than to that of heretics. There were also exiles for personal reasons. Giorgio Vasari, who rarely misses an opportunity to tell a good story, informs us that the sculptor Pietro Torrigiani of Florence had to leave town after a quarrel in which he had broken Michelangelo's nose. Had it not been for that brawl, the Henry VII chapel at Westminster might lack its fine Renaissance tomb. In the history of the Renaissance, as in history in general, one must never forget the importance of unintended consequences.

It is of course these consequences which make the visits of historical interest. Consequences such as the formal or informal instruction given by the visitors in Greek, or rhetoric, or poetry, or sculpture, or simply the encouragement to local talent to break with local tradition. At a chance meeting in Granada, in southern Spain, in 1526, Andrea Navagero, the Venetian ambassador, who happened to be a well-known poet, persuaded the Catalan Juan Boscán to write poems (in Castilian) in the Italian manner.

The cultural consequences of these visits were not always unintended. Some of the Italians went abroad because they had been invited by royal patrons such as François I, or by local aristocrats with literary or artistic interests, like Jan Zamojski, the chancellor of Poland in the later sixteenth century, who employed an Italian architect to design his new town, called Zamość after its founder [57]. The patrons themselves might be Italians living abroad in colonies of merchants in cities such as Bruges or Lyons. Italian princesses were also cultural intermediaries, the obvious examples being Beatrice of Aragon, from Naples, wife of King Mátyás of Hungary (Matthias Corvinus, who ruled 1458–90); Bona Sforza of Milan, who married King Zygmunt of Poland; and Catherine de' Medici, wife and widow of Henri II of France. Even soldiers might take an interest in art patronage; the painter Masolino was invited to Hungary by a Tuscan mercenary captain, Pippo Spano.

What were the local responses to these Italian migrants, their ideas and their skills? Some of them received an extremely warm welcome abroad. The Lombard humanist Pietro Martire Anghiera, for example, has left a famous account of his visit to the university of Salamanca in 1488, when he delivered a lecture on the Roman poet Juvenal. There were so many people in the audience that he could not get into the lecture-room until the beadle had cleared a passage with his staff, and when the visitor had given his lecture, he was carried off in triumph, so he tells us, like a victor at the Olympic games. Perhaps he was exaggerating the enthusiasm. Pietro Martire was, after all, a professional rhetorician. All the same, he had clearly had an experience worth describing to his patron. There were similar crowds, including members of the general public as well as students and teachers, to hear Girolamo Aleandro lecture on the poet Ausonius in Paris in 1511.

Other Italian humanists seem to have had a somewhat cooler reception abroad, if their itinerant careers are anything to go by.

Girolamo Balbo, for example, began by teaching in Paris, and moved on to the Netherlands, Germany and Bohemia, while Jacopo Publicio was active in Germany and Switzerland before settling down in Portugal. All the same, comparatively minor figures who had never been well known in Italy had the chance of turning into important people abroad, like Antonio Bonfini, who was a schoolmaster in the small town of Recanati before becoming court historian to Mátyás of Hungary. At this time, the late fifteenth century, Italian humanists were in particular demand because a local interest in classical literature and learning developed before there were native humanists to cater for it. A few years later, when the rising generation had been trained in humanism, it would be possible to do without these expatriates.

Another sign of indigenous interest in Renaissance culture in many parts of Europe is the traffic in the opposite direction. Of course the many visitors to Italy went for a number of different reasons. They did not all cross the Alps to meet scholars or look at paintings or old manuscripts or view the ruins of ancient Rome. As in the Middle Ages, diplomats, clerics, soldiers, merchants and pilgrims continued to make their way to Italy. Among the visitors with interests in Italian culture the largest group was that of the students, bound for two universities in particular, Bologna and Padua, to study two subjects, law and medicine. Law and medicine were not part of the *studia humanitatis*. They were gradually transformed under the influence of humanism, but we cannot assume that all the teachers approved of these innovations, and still less that the students (or their fathers, who paid for them), associated Italy with novelty in these respects.

Having made these qualifications, it is still possible to point to some well-documented visits to Italy which were made for what might be called good Renaissance reasons. Some artists went to Italy to study the new style of painting or the remains of classical sculpture and architecture. Albrecht Dürer, for example, was in Venice in 1505 and met a number of artists, including Giovanni Bellini, whom he described as 'still the best in painting' [108]. The Netherlander Jan van Scorel was in Italy in the 1520s, and his pupil Martin van Heemskerck (Plate 1)
lived in Rome in the 1530s, where he met Vasari as well as sketching ancient and modern buildings. The French architect Philbert de l'Orme was also in Rome in the 1530s.

For their part, scholars travelled to Italy to learn about texts and approaches unavailable at home. The two best known scientists, or natural philosophers, of the sixteenth century are probably Copernicus and Vesalius. Nicholas Copernicus, who came from Poland, studied Greek, mathematics and astronomy at the universities of Bologna, Padua and Ferrara at the end of the fifteenth century, studies which left many traces on his major work, *On the Revolutions of the Heavenly Orbs* (1543), which argued that the sun was at the centre of the universe [93]. Andreas Vesalius, who came from Flanders, went to the university of Padua to study medicine, including anatomy, the subject of his famous book *On the Fabric of the Human Body*, also published in 1543.

Another clear example of a scholar or writer visiting Italy for the sake of the new learning is that of Sir Thomas Hoby, a gentleman from Herefordshire best known for his English version of Castiglione's *Courtier*. Hoby's journal reveals that he went to Padua in 1548 to study Italian and 'humanitie', although he also attended lectures on logic and Roman law. Again, the Netherlander Justus Lipsius, one of the greatest scholars of the second half of the sixteenth century, went to Rome in 1567 in the retinue of his patron cardinal Granvelle in order to meet classical scholars, such as Carlo Sigonio, and to study the ancient world at first hand [70]. A third example is that of the French historian Jacques-Auguste de Thou, who recorded in his autobiography his 'passionate desire' to see Italy when he was twenty. On arrival in 1573 he bought ancient Greek texts in Venice and visited the picture collection at Mantua which had been formed by Isabella d'Este. He also met Vasari and Sigonio. A few years later, in 1580–1, it was the turn of Montaigne to visit Italy, where he admired the ruins of ancient Rome and looked at classical manuscripts in the Vatican library [113].

In many other cases, however, it was once again the unintended consequences which were important, the discovery of antiquity or the Renaissance by visitors who were not in search of them. For example, the German nobleman Ulrich von Hutten went to Italy to study law, but while he was there discovered the attractions of classical literature, in particular the satirical dialogues of Lucian, which served him as a model when he became involved in the polemics of the Reformation. Sir Thomas Wyatt seems to have discovered Italian poetry when he was on a diplo-

matic mission (as Geoffrey Chaucer had done long before in si- ↓
milar circumstances), and the example of Petrarch inspired his
own poems [78: ch. 12]. Wyatt's Spanish contemporary Garcilaso
de la Vega met the poets Luigi Tansillo and Bernardo Tasso (the
father of the more famous Torquato Tasso) in Naples, where he
had been banished for a misdemeanour. Like his friend Boscán
after his meeting with Navagero, Garcilaso wrote in a more Italian manner thereafter [74, pp. 194–8].

Of course the reception of the Renaissance cannot be reduced
to the movement of individuals. There was also the movement
of paintings and statues, like the works of art which François I .
of France, one of the great patrons of his time, ordered from
Florence [58]. There was the movement of books, the original
texts and the translations of Petrarch's poems, for example, of
Machiavelli's political writings, the treatise on architecture by
Bramante's pupil Sebastiano Serlio of Bologna (perhaps most influential through its illustrations), and so on.

In some respects, the reception of books (translations in particular) is easier to analyse than the more elusive personal relationships discussed so far. It is possible to discover how much was
translated, what was selected, what kinds of people made the
translations and most important of all, it is possible to chart the
popularity of particular texts via the number of editions and to
study in detail the changes made by the translators. The less
faithful the translations, the more valuable they are, in the sense
of offering more evidence about the process by which Italian
texts (and in some cases images) were adapted to the needs and
expectations of foreign readers. The reception of the Renaissance
– as of any alien system of values – was necessarily linked to its
perception, and perception is of course shaped by schemata. In
the sixteenth century, Italy was often viewed by foreigners as an
exotic country, the opposite of the perceiver's own culture. Translations help document the process of the domestication of this
dangerously attractive or attractively dangerous alien. The Italy
which the non-Italians imitated was to some extent their own invention, shaped by their needs and desires, just as the antiquity
which both they and the Italians aspired to imitate was in part
their construction.

Two examples may serve to illustrate this general process. The
first is the reception of Italian architecture abroad, while the

second, still more specific, is that of reactions outside Italy to Castiglione's *Courtier*.

Architecture seems especially relevant to the theme of 'the uses of Italy' because it is functional as well as decorative; because it obviously needs to be adapted to the local environment; and finally, because it is a collective art in which craftsmen as well as architects played a part. There were therefore many obstacles to the smooth diffusion abroad of designs made in Italy, despite the existence of famous pattern- books like the treatise by Serlio already mentioned, or Andrea Palladio's *Four Books of Architecture* (1570). Books of this kind were available in a number of European languages and could be studied by architects and patrons alike.

Even within Italy, however, local circumstances encouraged regional variation, so that the architecture of the Lombard or Venetian Renaissance was in many ways different from the Tuscan. These regional differences were sometimes exported with the Italian craftsmen who crossed the Alps. The Hungarians imitated the Tuscans, but French architecture tended to follow the Lombard model and German architecture the Venetian.

Italian Renaissance architecture has been described as spreading not as a 'total configuration', but in fragments [54]. We might reasonably speak of 're-employment' or 'bricolage', in this case the incorporation of new Italian elements into traditional local structures, particularly in the first phase of reception. In France in the early sixteenth century, for example, Italian decoration exerted more appeal than Italian ground-plans. In the case of the castle of Chambord, built for François I, the round towers are obviously traditional and only the architectural details are distinctively new [55: ch. 1]. Local stone was used because it was cheaper and also (as the French architect Philibert de l'Orme observed) more suitable to the climate. However, the material used necessarily affects the form. The architecture of Renaissance Italy was gradually acclimatised elsewhere.

In England too the imitation of Serlio, say, by the Elizabethan Robert Smythson, or of Palladio, by Inigo Jones, involved modifications for practical reasons as well as to express the architect's own creativity or the patron's self-image [61]. The modifications may not always have gone far enough, and caustic remarks have sometimes been made about the draughty porticos of English country houses which follow classical designs created for a Mediterranean climate. As Roger North wrote in the later seventeenth century, 'It hath been the use of the Italians, and ill imitated in England, by some fond surveyors, to set the portico into the house, as we find at Greenwich, the Queen's House. . . . In Italy this is proper and useful, because it abates heat and averts the force of the sun's light, which is offensive. . . . We have, generally speaking, too much air and too little heat, and therefore need not spoil an order of rooms to obtain the one and abate the other.' However, Sir Henry Wotton, in his *Elements of Architecture* (1624) already shows himself to be well aware of the problem of draughts, and also of the importance of items such as chimneys and steep roofs, which suited England better than Italy.

The implication of these examples is not that Italian designs were modified for utilitarian reasons alone. To say this would be to adopt the crude functionalism which I have been trying to avoid. The modifications came about for a variety of reasons. Some were obviously intentional, others less so. In some cases, the divergences from Italian models were the result of the employment of local craftsmen who had their own traditions and were unable or unwilling to understand what was being asked of them. Chambord, for example, designed for François I by an Italian architect, Domenico da Cortona, was actually built by French masons. The new town of Zamość in Poland was planned by an Italian, Bernardo Morando, but the plans were once again carried out by local craftsmen. A spectacular example of the conflict and the interpenetration of local traditions and Italian models can be seen in the architecture of the Renaissance in Spain, where in the south at least, the craft tradition of Islam – the so-called *mudejar* style – was still strong.

On occasion it was the patron (who was still very much in control) who demanded modifications to Italian designs for symbolic reasons rather than utilitarian ones. At the end of the fifteenth century, Tsar Ivan III of Russia asked an Italian, Aristotile Fioravanti, to design the cathedral of St Michael's at the Kremlin. However, he required Fioravanti to follow the plan of the twelfth-century cathedral at Vladimir [59: ch. 1]. In other words, he was aware of the prestige of Italian artists, but unwilling to break with architectural traditions which were linked to religious ones.

The tsar's ambivalent attitude to the west is an extreme case of a reaction to Italian culture which was not uncommon at this time. For a variety of reasons, then, what we find is not the simple export of Italian models abroad but their reconstruction, and the development of hybrid forms which may be described as misunderstandings (from the sender's point of view) or creative adaptations (from the point of view of the receivers).

At this point it may be useful to turn to our second concrete example. As a printed guide to action, to the construction of the self, Castiglione's *Courtier* had a status not unlike that of the architectural treatises of Serlio and Palladio. The diffusion, translation and imitation of this book has therefore a good deal to tell us about the adoption and the assimilation of the Italian model of behaviour for both gentlemen and ladies – the third book of the *Courtier* discusses the qualities of the ideal lady-in-waiting [19, 86, 106].

Castiglione's dialogue was published for the first time in 1528 and it was quickly translated into Spanish and French and a little later into Latin, English, and German. The Spanish translator was Juan Boscán and the English translator was Sir Thomas Hoby. Their enthusiasm for Italian culture has already been discussed, but it may be of interest to add that each of them was encouraged to make the translation by a lady of their acquaintance. The point which needs to be emphasised in an account of the reception of the Renaissance, however, is the difficulty of rendering the Italian text into other languages.

For example, Hoby claimed to have attempted, as he put it, 'to follow the very meaning and words of the author, without being misled by fantasy, or leaving out any parcel one or other'. However, at this time the English language lacked precise equivalents for some of Castiglione's key concepts, forcing Hoby to coin new terms. *Cortegiania* itself, which we might render today as 'courtiership', was paraphrased as 'the trade and manner of courtiers'. The famous concept of *sprezzatura*, a sort of careless grace, was rendered either by 'disgracing' or by 'recklessness'. It is not clear – to me at least – why Hoby did not use the word 'negligence' which Chaucer had used before him and which corresponds to the *negligentia* of Castiglione's own model, the ancient Roman Cicero. The point to emphasise, though, is that the lack of English equivalents for Castiglione's keywords suggests that the diffusion of his ideas could not be smooth, despite the fact that the institution of the court was familiar enough in England, France, Spain and elsewhere.

1. A northern artist in Rome: Martin van Heemskerck.

2. The High Renaissance: Bramante's *Tempietto*.

3. Antiquity reconstructed: Botticelli's version of the *Calumny* of Apelles.

4. Antiquity reconstructed II: Michelangelo's *Bacchus*.

5. A classical paradigm: the Pantheon in Rome.

6. A humanist view of the world: Bouelles.

Similar points could be made about the French and Spanish translations. Still more revealing, however, because it is still further from the original, is the Polish version of the *Courtier* the *Dworzanin Polski*, published in 1566 by Lukasz Górnicki. It is not so much a translation as a transposition. The setting, for example, is moved from the court of Urbino in 1508 to that of a villa near Cracow in 1550. The controversies over the best form of Italian to speak and write are translated into comparisons between the various Slav languages. All the roles in the dialogue are taken by Polish noblemen, women being eliminated on the grounds that they are not learned enough – in Poland – to take part in conversations about literature, philosophy and so on. Górnicki also declares that he is going to leave out Castiglione's discussion of the arts of painting and sculpture because 'we don't know about them here'.

In the strict sense of the term the *Dworzanin Polski* is an unreliable translation. However, given the views on imitation expressed in the *Courtier* itself – notably the idea that if we imitate the ancients we do not imitate them, because they did not imitate anyone – it might be argued that Górnicki was a more faithful translator than Hoby (say), precisely because he was less faithful. He was doing his best to translate Italian culture into Polish terms, and to translate the culture he had to take liberties with the text. His elimination of women, for example, was not arbitrary but rather an expression of the gap – or gulf – between the two cultures. This example may serve as a useful reminder of the social obstacles (no less serious than linguistic or climatic obstacles) to any simple diffusion of Italian values abroad.

So do the foreign attacks on Castiglione or on the young men and women who aspired to behave like the characters in his dialogue. They express an anti-Italian backlash, a hostility to what one is tempted to call Italian cultural imperialism, disguised as a defence of sincerity. The English poet John Marston, for example, satirised 'the absolute Castilio' and his 'ceremonious compliment'. In France, Castiglione was associated with dissimulation and with the 'corruption' of the French language by the influx of new words derived from the Italian, a process which irritated the critics themselves into coining such new terms as 'italianization' [86].

There were similar attacks on Machiavelli, who was also associated with dissimulation and who was suspected of 'atheism' into the bargain. As the figure of 'Machiavel' explains in the prologue to Christopher Marlowe's *The Jew of Malta* (*c.*1591),

> I count religion but a childish toy,
> And hold there is no sin but ignorance.

This hostile reaction to Machiavelli, Castiglione and other writers was not merely anti-Italian. It was also anti-Catholic, or in the language of the day, 'anti-Papist'. Yet another obstacle to the smooth diffusion of the Italian Renaissance abroad was the Reformation.

There is or was a common view that the major difference between the Renaissance north of the Alps and the movement in Italy itself was the rise of 'christian humanism', associated with Erasmus in particular. This view rests on the assumption – a false assumption, so it was suggested in section 2 above – that Italy was full of 'pagan' humanists, to whom the pious northerners may be contrasted. In fact, as we have seen, the leaders of the Italian movement – Valla, for example, and Ficino – were concerned with divinity as well as with the humanities, and they made a conscious effort to harmonise their devotion to antiquity with their Christianity, just as some of the Fathers of the Church had done. Indeed, they may reasonably be described as devoted to two antiquities, that of the Fathers as well as that of the classics [49].

What can be affirmed with more confidence is that the humanist movement north of the Alps was even more concerned with sacred studies than its Italian counterpart and predecessor [64; 102: ch. 14]. This was not because the northerners were better Christians. The contrast was partly a result of the different institutional base of the northern movement (more closely associated with universities and even monasteries than had been the case in Italy), and partly a result of the timing, which coincided with the movement for the reform of the Church (before as well as after Martin Luther).

The model northern humanist was of course Erasmus, who lived from about 1466 to 1536 [109]. Erasmus was deeply interested in the classics, but in his thirties he turned to more Christian studies. He spent a good deal of time on the textual criticism and translation of the Bible (going back to the original

Greek version of the New Testament), and he also edited some of the Fathers of the Church, including Jerome and Origen [68]. In some of his own writings he tried, like them, to harmonise christian with classical ideas. For example, in one of his dialogues, *The Godly Feast*, one speaker describes Cicero as 'divinely inspired', while another refers to the effectively Christian sentiments of Socrates, leading a third to declare that he 'can hardly help exclaiming, St Socrates, pray for us!'

All the same, tension remained between the christian and the classical, as a still more famous dialogue of Erasmus reveals. This is the *Ciceronianus* (1528), the title of which recalls Jerome's guilty dream. The protagonist of the dialogue, a certain Nosoponus, wants to write Latin exactly like Cicero. Another speaker objects that this would be impossible without bringing back the Rome of Cicero, thus underlining the paradox of imitation (by imitating the ancients in a changed world, we are not imitating them), and illustrating the Renaissance sense of the past, the new sensitivity to anachronism. However, the main theme of the dialogue is that Cicero should not be imitated because he was a pagan. One speaker criticises the Latin epic on the nativity written by the Italian poet Jacopo Sannazzaro on the grounds that he should have treated a sacred subject in a less classicizing, less Virgilian manner. Someone tells the story of a sermon before Julius II which compared the pope to the pagan god Jupiter [21]. In other words, the idea that Italian humanism was pagan goes back at least as far as Erasmus. All the same, it seems to be based on misinformation, reflecting misunderstandings and cultural distance between North and South. Recent research on preaching in the pope's chapel failed to discover the sermon to which Erasmus objected.

The early sixteenth century was the most important moment of interaction between the humanist movement and religious studies. It was in 1508 that a 'trilingual' college was founded in Alcalá, in Spain, to study the three languages of the Bible: Hebrew, Greek and Latin [68: ch. 3]. The Spanish humanist Juan Luis Vives edited Augustine and advocated the study in schools of the second antiquity, in other words of early Christian rather than pagan writers. In France, the theologian Jacques Lefèvre d'Etaples learned Greek to study the New Testament and the neoplatonic writers in the original language. In Germany, Johan

Reuchlin, a specialist in Hebrew, was the most famous member of a group of humanists with theological interests. In London, Erasmus's friend John Colet put early Christian writers such as Lactantius and the poet Juvencus onto the syllabus of his new school at St Paul's [102: ch. 15]. In Cambridge, the Professor of Greek, John Cheke, translated the great preacher John Chrysostom, bishop of Constantinople, as well as the ancient Greek tragedian Euripides.

The association between humanism and theology was at its height in the first two decades of the sixteenth century, before the excommunication of Luther and his conflict with Erasmus, but it did not disappear thereafter. What we see might be better described as the adaptation to new circumstances of humanist ideas and humanist skills. When humanism was defined, as it used to be, in terms of the 'dignity of man', Luther was viewed as an anti-humanist because (unlike Pico, say, or Erasmus) he did not believe in free will. However, he was no enemy of humanism in the sense of the *studia humanitatis*. He had had a classical education himself and he was sympathetic to the scholarly revival of ancient learning, which he believed to have been encouraged by God as a preparation for the reform of the Church. He supported his colleague Philip Melanchthon's efforts to give the university of Wittenberg a humanist syllabus [71: ch. 9; 72: ch. 6; 73: ch. 4].

As for the other reformers, Zwingli was even closer to the humanists than Luther was, and believed that some of the virtuous pagans, such as Socrates, had been saved. Calvin was more ambivalent. He was suspicious of what he called *les sciences humaines* – in other words, the humanities – as 'vain curiosity'. On the other hand, he had participated in these studies in his youth, commenting on a text by the Roman philosopher Seneca, and even in his maturity he did not reject Cicero and Plato altogether. On the contrary, he quoted from them frequently in his *Institutes of the Christian Religion*. It was not such a paradox as it may seem, then, that one of the leading figures in humanist education outside Italy should have been the French Calvinist scholar Petrus Ramus [45: ch. 7]

In Catholic Europe too the association between religious studies and the humanist movement outlasted the Reformation. It even outlasted the Council of Trent, although the humanists suffered a major defeat at the Council in the early 1560s, in their attempts to replace the Vulgate, the official Latin version of the Bible, with a new translation from the original Greek and Hebrew. The notorious Index of Prohibited Books, which was made official and applied to the whole Church by the Council of Trent, included the works of Erasmus, which was another defeat for the humanists. Erasmus was now accused of laying the eggs which Luther hatched.

On the other hand, the Index did not ban classical literature, which remained an important part of the syllabus of the Catholic grammar schools, those of the Jesuits in particular. It is commonly said that the Jesuits favoured the letter but not the spirit of humanism, but this interpretation depends to a large extent on the discredited view that 'real' humanists were essentially pagan or worldly. The Jesuit adaptation of the classical tradition to the needs of Catholic boys in the second half of the sixteenth century differed in details but not in fundamentals from earlier attempts by Erasmus and Colet. It was not even so very different from the curricula devised by early humanist schoolmasters such as Vittorino da Feltre and Guarino da Verona. The main difference between humanist teachers and Jesuit teachers was that the first group rejected medieval philosophy while the second accepted it [46; 102: ch. 16].

Just as some of the clergy tried to combine the techniques of humanism with those of medieval philosophy, so we find nobles attempting to fuse humanism with the traditional attitudes and values of a military aristocracy, so that historians have had to invent hybrid terms like 'learned chivalry' or 'chivalric humanism' to describe the combination, whether in the courts of northern Italy (such as Ariosto's Ferrara), in fifteenth-century Burgundy, or in England under the Tudors [69]. Count Baldassare Castiglione, for example, the Spanish soldier-poet Garcilaso de la Vega and Sir Philip Sidney all preached and practised not only the new values associated with the Renaissance but also the traditional virtues of medieval knights − skill in warfare, chivalry and courtesy. The combination of old and new is particularly striking in the 'Accession Day Tilts' in the reign of Queen Elizabeth, in which knights, including Sidney, decorated their equipment with Renaissance devices but fought in late medieval style, thus enacting the chivalric humanism which found its literary expression in the *Faerie Queene* of Sidney's friend Edmund Spenser [65].

One example after another prompts the generalisation that (like many other attempts at reform or renewal) the humanist movement became less radical and less distinctive as it became more successful. The history of political thought would seem to confirm this conclusion. The humanist movement grew up in the environment of the city-states of north and central Italy, shaping it and being shaped by it, as the example of Leonardo Bruni and the Florentine struggle with Milan, discussed above, illustrates [43, 44]. The state most closely associated with humanism, Florence, remained a republic in name at least until 1530, although the writings of Machiavelli and his friend Guicciardini suggest that the old confidence in reason and in human nature was shattered in 1494 when the Florentines proved unable to resist the invading forces of Charles VIII of France [48: ch. 3]. In Florence and in other republics, notably Venice and Genoa (both of which retained this form of government until the late eighteenth century), it was not difficult for the ruling class, and the humanists associated with it, to identify with the men who had governed the ancient republics of Athens and Rome, especially with Cicero, who had combined the roles of politician, orator and philosopher [67; 104: chs 4–9].

This humanist republicanism or 'civic humanism', as it is often called, also exercised a certain appeal in some of the free cities of Germany and Switzerland. This was true of sixteenth- century Basel, for example, or of Nuremberg, where the town council included such men as Willibald Pirckheimer, who was a friend of the artist Albrecht Dürer and a translator of Greek classics such as Plutarch and Lucian. Erasmus, who came from Rotterdam, one of the more or less independent cities of the Netherlands, and spent a good deal of time in Basel, was sympathetic to republics and often critical of princes. He once declared that princes are rightly compared to eagles because that bird is greedy, rapacious and bloodthirsty. He may well have been thinking of the emperor Maximilian, whose symbol was the double-headed eagle and who had recently attempted to squeeze more tax revenue from the Low Countries [109].

Elsewhere in Europe, on the other hand, monarchy was the norm, and so the examples of classical or modern Italian republics had little practical relevance. This was the world of the so-called 'Renaissance prince'. The term is a convenient one, but unfortunately it is also somewhat ambiguous. If historians describe the emperor Charles V, for example, or François I, or Henry VIII in this way, they may mean that these princes took an interest in humanism and the arts, or that they governed in a new way (perhaps connected to the cultural changes of the time), or simply that they lived in the period which we call 'the Renaissance'.

In the first sense of the term, there was no shortage of Renaissance princes, or indeed princesses such as Marguerite de Navarre (the sister of François I, active as a writer as well as a patron) or Mary of Hungary (sister of Charles V, and the patron of a number of artists). Charles himself commissioned paintings from Titian, and even took artists on campaign to record his exploits. Henry VIII employed Holbein, while François, as we have seen, called Italian artists to court and built on a grand scale at Chambord and Fontainebleau. The king's patronage of scholars, notably his foundation of the 'royal lecturers' in Greek and Hebrew, was extremely important in the establishment of humanism in France [58].

On the other hand, historians have become rather sceptical of the claim that these and other monarchs governed in a new, 'Renaissance' manner, and now tend to emphasise the survival of late medieval traditions of administration. The essential relation between politics and the spread of the Renaissance is one of a rather different kind. The political culture of northern Europe helped to determine what was taken either from the classical tradition or from contemporary Italy. For example, it was its relevance to societies on the other side of the Alps as well as its own literary merits which made Castiglione's *Courtier* so popular outside Italy. Although Machiavelli served the Florentine Republic, and wrote his *Discourses* on the early history of Rome for the instructions of his fellow- citizens in particular, outside Italy he was best known − or most notorious − for his little book of advice to princes. Thomas More may have been inspired to write his *Utopia* by the example of Plato's *Republic*, but it was the problems of the kingdom of England under Henry VIII with which he was most concerned [67: ch. 9; 114]. Erasmus too, whatever he thought of eagles, wrote a book on *The Education of a Christian Prince* for the benefit of the young Charles V, advising him, among other things, that if he found that he could not rule without injustice or the destruction of religion, then he should resign. Erasmus may well have had a classical precedent in mind, that of the Roman emperor Diocletian. However, his suggestion was to become more topical than he could have foreseen. In the year 1555 Charles did resign, following a civil war in his empire in which religious issues – Protestantism versus Catholicism – played an important part. Had the emperor been thinking of the advice given him by Erasmus forty years earlier?

Charles's court preacher, the Spanish friar Antonio de Guevara, was also involved in the humanist movement and he turned his admonitions into the form of a treatise called *The Dial of Princes*, which drew heavily on the Roman moralist Seneca and held up before Charles the example of the philosopher-emperor Marcus Aurelius. Guevara's work, which was often reprinted and translated into English, French, and other languages, is a famous example of Renaissance neostoicism. Another is the treatise *On Constancy* published by the Flemish humanist Justus Lipsius in 1584 [70]. What attracted sixteenth-century readers in the Greek and Roman stoic philosophers, Seneca in particular, was their advice on preserving tranquillity of mind or 'constancy' in the face of tyranny, death, or what Hamlet called 'the slings and arrows of outrageous fortune'. As an inscription on a sixteenth-century English portrait puts it,

> More than a rock amidst the raging seas,
> The constant heart no danger dreads nor fears.

In similar fashion Pamela, the heroine of Sidney's pastoral romance *Arcadia*, is described as standing firm 'like a rock amidst the sea, beaten both with the winds and with the waves, yet itself immovable'. The essentially passive virtue of constancy was more appropriate for the subjects of a monarch than for the politically active citizens of a republic.

As in the case of stoic philosophy, the revival or reception of Roman law – the law of the Roman Empire, rather than that of the Republic – became particularly important in the monarchies north of the Alps. Roman law had been studied during the Middle Ages, in the university of Bologna in particular. In the fifteenth and sixteenth centuries, however, scholars became increasingly aware of the relation between this law and the society which had produced it, and also of the changes in the legal system in the course of time. A number of Italian humanists took a philological interest in ancient legal texts, but from the lawyer's point of view they were amateurs. The real advances were made by men with a double training, in law as well as in the humanities. Of the three leading figures in the reinterpretation of Roman law in the early sixteenth century, only one, Andrea Alciati, was an Italian, and he spent much of his life teaching in France, at the universities of Avignon and Bourges. Guillaume Budé was a Parisian, while Ulrich Zasius, who was a friend of Erasmus, came from the German city of Constance. If the first humanists to study Roman law were Italians, it was the French who made the greatest contribution in the long run [66]. This was appropriate enough, since French monarchs claimed, as Roman emperors had done, to be 'absolute', in other words above the laws, and it was a Roman jurist who declared that 'what pleases the prince has the force of law'.

A very different sphere in which northern or western Europeans are generally held to have surpassed their Italian masters is that of prose fiction. In the case of comedy, it was difficult to do better than Ariosto and Aretino (though Shakespeare rose to the challenge). In the epic, it was hard to outdo Ariosto (which was Spenser's aim in the *Faerie Queene*); in the pastoral, to improve on Tasso's *Aminta* or Gianbattista Guarini's *Pastor Fido* (1585), a romantic play about a faithful lover, which was much imitated all over Europe at the turn of the century. In the case of prose fiction (it is misleading to use the term 'novel'), the Italians from Boccaccio to Bandello were masters of the short story. However, the development of the genre into something more ambitious took place outside Italy. The great masters of the new form were of course François Rabelais, with his *Pantagruel* (1532), *Gargantua* (1534), and the *Tiers Livre* (1546), and Miguel de Cervantes, with his *Don Quixote* (in two parts, 1605 and 1615). Comparatively minor figures also produced work of high quality, from Sir Philip Sidney's *Arcadia* (originally written *c*.1580), one of a European series of pastoral romances, to the anonymous Spanish *Lazarillo de Tormes* (1554), which broke with convention by telling the story of a professional beggar and trickster from the point of view of this unheroic hero [74: part 4].

45

These works of fiction owe a considerable debt to classical antiquity. To the comic dialogues of Lucian, which had already inspired Hutten and Erasmus; to the ancient Greek romances, such as *Daphnis and Chloe*; and above all to late Latin prose fiction, to the *Golden Ass* of Apuleius and to the *Satyricon* of Petronius. However, what Rabelais and Cervantes actually produced is without parallel. One of the most novel features in the work of both men was the importance of parody, the parody of medieval romances of chivalry in particular, going further than the ambiguous, ironic treatment of chivalry in Ariosto's *Orlando Furioso*. A major theme in the romances was the quest for the grail; the heroes of Rabelais, on the other hand, undertake a kind of anti-quest for the 'Oracle of the Holy Bacbuc', which takes the form of a bottle (the praise of drinking is a recurrent theme in Rabelais). As for Don Quixote, who is described on the very first page as a compulsive reader of romances of chivalry, his adventures are a comic transposition of the stories of knights errant with which his head is full.

Another novel feature in both stories is the discussion in the text itself of the problem of interpretation, the relation between fiction and reality. In the prologue to *Gargantua* the author (not Rabelais but a certain 'Master Alcofribas', according to the title page) suggests that the comic story contains a serious kernel, though he goes on to confuse the issue by making fun of people who find allegorical meanings in the poems of Homer [76, 77, 117]. Cervantes too claims not to be inventing a story, but to be retelling what he found in the work of an Arab historian, while Don Quixote himself enacts the problems of interpretation by his persistence in treating windmills as enemy knights and ordinary life as if it were a romance of chivalry [107].

It has sometimes been suggested that this ironic self-consciousness was encouraged by the rise of the printed book, and that it is 'print culture' which explains the main differences between Renaissance writers and those of the Middle Ages. Indeed, it has been claimed that without printing there would have been no Renaissance at all [133]. The point is an important one, although easy to exaggerate or misinterpret. Since the invention of printing with movable type goes back only as far as the mid-fifteenth century, it is clear that it cannot have influenced the early Renaissance: the ideas of Petrarch and Alberti, the painting of

Giotto and Masaccio, the architecture and the perspective of Brunelleschi. However, it is equally clear that the so-called 'diffusion' of the Renaissance was greatly facilitated by the new technology. In the case of architecture, the importance of printed treatises by Vitruvius, Serlio, Palladio and others in spreading the knowledge of classical forms has already been stressed. Again, the fashion for the love-lyrics of Petrarch in aristocratic circles in the sixteenth century is almost inconceivable (on this scale, at least) without the presence of the elegant little volumes printed in italic type which young men and women can be seen to be holding in many painted portraits of the time [75]. Most obvious and most important of all is the stimulus to the revival of classical antiquity provided by the printing of the Greek and Roman writers.

A crucial role in this movement of revival was played by a group of scholar-printers in Italy, France, the Netherlands, Switzerland and elsewhere, who acted as middlemen between humanist scholars and the educated public. The great reputation enjoyed by Erasmus in his own day would have been inconceivable without the aid of print and printers such as Aldus Manutius of Venice or the Amerbachs and Frobens of Basel, whom he numbered among his friends. Aldus, for example, had studied the humanities at Ferrara and his elegant editions of Greek texts in the original language expressed a personal enthusiasm for the classics.

However, the place of print in the Renaissance was more than that of an agent of diffusion, important as this function was. It is hard to imagine how the textual criticism of the humanists discussed above could have been developed until there was a means of preserving as well as making emendations to texts. More generally, it has been argued that if the Carolingian Renaissance and the twelfth-century Renaissance burned themselves out in a relatively short time, while 'the' Renaissance lasted so much longer, the success of the latter must be attributed largely to print [125, 133]. There is an obvious parallel with the history of unorthodox ideas. The Reformation succeeded where medieval heresies had failed because it had access to a mass-produced medium for the propagation of new ideas.

Of course the Reformation did not spread by print alone, but by word of mouth as well, and the same can be said of the

Renaissance. Small but influential discussion groups like the Platonic Academy in Florence or the Palace Academy of Henri III of France are a reminder of the importance of orality in learned culture. The dialogue, one of the most important literary forms of the period (think of the *Colloquies* of Erasmus, More's *Utopia*, and so on) was often modelled on actual discussions, and its style combines literary elements with what has been called 'oral residue', so that it is hard to say whether orality is being assimilated by print, or print by orality.

Again, some of the literary masterpieces of the Renaissance draw inspiration from traditional popular culture, which was an oral culture. The *Praise of Folly* by Erasmus, for example, draws on a popular tradition of feasts of fools as well as on St Paul and the classical tradition of satire. In *Don Quixote*, Sancho Panza in particular belongs to a popular comic tradition. 'Panza' means 'paunch', and Sancho's rotundity makes him reminiscent of the figure of Carnival, while his tall thin master resembles Lent. Another carnivalesque figure from head to toe (or, since he cannot see his toes, from head to belly) is Falstaff, and his abandonment by Prince Hal has been compared to the 'trial of Carnival', a ritual with which the festive season often closed. Still more thoroughly carnivalesque are the *Gargantua* and the *Pantagruel* of Rabelais: the giants, the trickster Panurge, the stress on feasting, drinking and defecating, the comedy of violence, and the use of the hyperbolic language of mountebanks [76]. The point is not to argue that Rabelais was a popular writer; he was a learned man, a physician well-read in Greek and Latin literature and an admirer of Erasmus, and his book is full of allusions which would have been unintelligible to the craftsmen of Lyons (where his book was first published) or to the local peasants [117]. What Rabelais does is to appropriate popular culture for his own purposes, for example to mock the traditional learned culture of the hide-bound theologians of the Sorbonne. The use of popular forms for subversive purposes was particularly frequent in the late Renaissance, the phase of disintegration, which the following section will discuss.

48

4   The Disintegration of the Renaissance

If it is difficult to decide when the Renaissance began, it is quite impossible to say when it ended. Some scholars have chosen the 1520s, while the majority opt for 1600, 1620, 1630 or even later. It is always hard to say when a movement has come to an end, and this is doubly difficult when so many regions and arts are involved. 'End' is too sharp, too decisive a word in this case. A better term might be 'disintegration'. The point is that what began as a movement of a few people with clear aims gradually lost its unity as it spread, so that in the course of time it becomes more and more difficult to decide who or what belongs to it.

In the visual arts, in Italy, the 1520s mark the transition from the High Renaissance to what art historians now call 'Mannerism', a tendency (rather than an organised movement) to place unusual emphasis on 'manner' or style; on novelty, difficulty, ingenuity, elegance and wit [99]. It was, for instance, in the 1520s that work began on Michelangelo's Medici Chapel in Florence, the building described by the artist's pupil Vasari as 'extremely novel' because 'he departed a great deal from the kind of architecture regulated by proportion, order and rule that other artists made according to common usage and following Vitruvius and the works of antiquity'. Michelangelo rejected the classical orders, for example, for forms of his own. Towards the end of the same decade, Giulio Romano also broke the rules in his Palazzo de Te in Mantua; indeed, his deliberately 'ungrammatical' combinations of classical elements seem to have been intended to shock the spectator in a playful kind of way. They are in a sense 'anti-classical', although there were actually precedents for this kind of rule-breaking in late classical antiquity itself [36: chs 7 and 9].

49

In the case of painting and sculpture it is less easy to decide what should count as 'mannerist'. A rejection of the rules of proportion and perspective can be found in the paintings of Rosso, Pontormo and Parmigianino in the 1520s and 1530s, associated with a rather cold elegance which can also be seen in the portraits of Pontormo's pupil Bronzino. A similar rejection of the conventions, associated this time with expressive force, can be found in Michelangelo's *Last Judgement* (1536–41) in the Sistine Chapel. The artist is said to have remarked that all the rules of proportion and perspective are of no use 'without the eye', an idea which was elaborated into a theory by Giovan Paolo Lomazzo later in the century. In the case of sculpture, elongated figures in elegantly twisted poses ('snakelike', *figura serpentinata*, as Michelangelo called them) are the main criteria of the mannerist phase, which is usually taken to include Cellini's statue of Perseus and the salt-cellar he made for François I (both works of the 1540s), and Bartolommeo Ammanati's *Fountain of Neptune* in the Piazza della Signoria in Florence [33: chs 10–11]. The playful side of Mannerism is well exemplified in the art of gardens and grottoes (from which the term 'grotesque' is derived); the Boboli Gardens in Florence, for example, or the park at Bomarzo designed for the Roman aristocrat Vicino Orsini, which takes the form of a sixteenth-century Disneyland complete with stone monsters, a leaning tower, and a hell mouth inside which can be found a marble picnic table [41].

The examples quoted so far, apart from Parmigianino, are Tuscan or Roman. In Venice, by contrast, Titian and his followers continued to work in the High Renaissance style in the 1520s and beyond. Tintoretto's absorption of a Michelangelesque style can be seen in his dramatic *St Mark Rescuing a Slave* of 1548, in which the saint hurtles downward like a Renaissance Superman, but Palladio followed the classical rules in the villas he was designing in the 1550s and 1560s, and Veronese too went on working in the High Renaissance manner until his death in 1588.

In literature it is still more difficult, and also less fruitful, to try to decide who was a mannerist and who was not. It is tempting to take Michelangelo's poems, Vasari's *Lives* and Cellini's autobiography as examples of literary mannerism because of what we know about the other activities of their authors. The pastoral dramas of Tasso and Guarini are also common choices. These pieces are certainly self-conscious and stylish; the problem is that the same adjectives also apply to many earlier works of Renaissance literature. Guarini was criticised for trying to combine two genres, tragedy and pastoral, but the other works just mentioned do not flout the rules in the manner of Pontormo or Giulio Romano. They are not anti-classical. Music too poses a problem. The madrigals of the late sixteenth-century Sicilian prince Carlo Gesualdo are often described as 'mannerist', but the development of music was, as we have seen, out of phase with that of the other arts.

To identify mannerist works outside Italy is also difficult. The main problem stems from the fact that although the 1520s were late in the career of the Renaissance in Italy, they were early in that movement's history in France, Spain, England, and central and eastern Europe (apart from Hungary in the late fifteenth century). Hence an ungrammatical building like the palace built at Heidelberg in the 1550s, known after its patron as the Otthein-richbau, may be the result either of ignorance or of sophistication [59: ch. 6]. A case can be made for dating Mannerism relatively early in the Netherlands, where artists were relatively well-informed about trends elsewhere, but the best known and least disputed examples of the tendency outside Italy are as late as the 1580s, when El Greco began working for Philip II of Spain – who preferred Titian – while Bartolomaeus Spranger entered the service of the emperor Rudolf II [101].

As for attempts to find literary mannerism outside Italy, they have little use except to reveal the latent ambiguities of the concept. Some critics would choose John Lyly's *Euphues* (1579) as a typical example, a romance written in a manner so deliberately idiosyncratic and so widely imitated that the term 'euphuism' had to be invented to describe it. Others would choose the poetry and prose of John Donne, whose style was a reaction against euphuism. Again, the essays of Montaigne are sometimes discussed as 'Renaissance' productions, sometimes as part of a 'Counter--Renaissance', and sometimes as mannerist or even as 'baroque'. It seems more useful to make the more modest points that whatever we call him, Montaigne could not have done what he did had the earlier Renaissance not taken place, but that he does not and could not share all the values of the late Renaissance, an age of variety in which artists and writers went off in different

51

directions. His relaxed style of writing was not artless (as it claimed to be) but it did not break with the classical tradition. It expressed a not uncommon reaction of the time against the dignified and complex sentences of Cicero, and in favour of the more informal style of Seneca. This deceptively simple style was also appropriate for a writer who maintained a detached, sceptical attitude in the face of the pretensions of kings and scholars and of grand claims for human dignity and the power of reason [113].

Whether we find the term 'Mannerism' useful, or prefer to use the more neutral 'Late Renaissance', the changes which took place after c.1530 or so require explanation. The explanations commonly given are of two opposite (though possibly complementary) kinds. In the first place, there are what may be called 'internalist' accounts, explanations in terms of the internal history or internal 'logic' of a particular genre. If we think of the history of Renaissance painting, as Vasari did, as the progressively more successful imitation of nature, then we may well wonder what could possibly follow the apogee of Leonardo, Raphael and early Michelangelo. If we think of the history of Renaissance architecture as the progressively more correct imitation of the rules of the ancients, a similar problem arises after the High Renaissance. Where could one go from there? In any artistic or literary tradition there usually comes a time when it is perceived by its practitioners as exhausted, when a need to react against it is felt. In such a late phase, the public – spectators, readers, listeners – are likely to be more conscious of the conventions than their predecessors were, and thus to appreciate the allusiveness and wit of artists who are wilfully incorrect, who subvert or play with the rules.

In the second place, there are the 'externalist' explanations of changes in culture as a response to changes in society. In the case of Mannerism, the response is generally described in terms of 'crisis', whether the crisis identified is religious, political or social. It was, of course, in the 1520s that Luther broke with the Church of Rome, while in 1527 the city of Rome was sacked by the army of Charles V [100]. These were traumatic events for many Italians, though not necessarily more traumatic than the 1490s, the decade of Savonarola's call for the reform of the Church and the French invasion of Italy. We know that Michelangelo took his religion very seriously and that he was tormented by doubts about his salvation. It is plausible enough to suggest relationships between his religious paintings and his religious ideas; rather less plausible to explain his architectural innovations in the same way [112]. Cellini's autobiography, on the other hand, does not give the impression that its hero passed through a religious crisis, or even that he found the Sack of Rome traumatic; he seems to have enjoyed it as an adventure. All the same, he sculpted in the new style. Again, the stiff elegance of the men and women portrayed by Pontormo or Bronzino is sometimes treated as a symptom of 'alienation' (whether the artist's or the sitter's), but it may simply have been an attempt to render a currently fashionable Spanish style of aloof aristocratic behaviour. Generally speaking, so little is known about the inner lives of most artists in this period that it is unwise to make assumptions one way or the other.

Was Mannerism a response to a social crisis? Social crises are always difficult to define, let alone date, but there is at least evidence of a change in the social and political structure. In sixteenth-century Italy there does seem to have been a gradual shift of wealth and power away from merchants and towards the landowning class, a shift which Marxists describe as 'refeudalisation' [7]. The independent city-states and their merchant patriciates were replaced – Venice and Genoa apart – by courts and aristocracies. Elegant, sophisticated, playful and allusive, Mannerism is an aristocratic style [99].

Mannerism is sometimes characterised as an 'anti-Renaissance' or 'Counter-Renaissance', but it might be better to describe it as a late phase of the Renaissance, since the breaking of the classic rules was not meant altogether seriously and in any case it assumed a knowledge of the very rules which were broken. If we turn to the humanists of the time, the scholars and the men of letters, we find that they were concerned not to break with the Renaissance past but rather to elaborate some aspects of it at the expense of others. Political writers such as Giovanni Botero, whose *Reason of State* (1589) did a good deal to make that term fashionable, continued to comment on Roman history, but now turned to Tacitus on the late Empire rather than Livy on the early Republic. 'Neoplatonism', as the cult of Plato is generally called, became fashionable in court circles in sixteenth-century Europe, from Paris to Prague, perhaps because a stress on the contemplative rather than on the active life suited the subjects of monarchies (as opposed to the citizens of republics). The neoplatonic movement involved an interest not only in the writings of Plato himself, but also in those of his late classical followers such as Plotinus and Iamblichus, who had turned increasingly to mysticism and magic. There seems to have been an increasing concern with the 'occult philosophy' (as we would say, 'magic') and with 'natural philosophy' (in modern terms, 'science'), perhaps because these studies – which it was not yet possible to distinguish – offered an escape from the troubled world of humanity. The Polish canon Nicolaus Copernicus, the German Heinrich Cornelius Agrippa, the Englishman John Dee and the Italian Giordano Bruno (burned for heresy in Rome in 1600), were among the most famous of those who took this route [50, 53, 73, 92].

Another response to crisis was the stoic revival discussed in section 3 above. The cult of constancy seems to have been at the height of its appeal in the second half of the sixteenth century, when the civil wars in France and the Netherlands made the tranquillity of mind recommended by Seneca and other stoic philosophers as necessary as it was difficult to attain. Others, like Montaigne, who became disillusioned with stoicism, turned to classical scepticism, to the doctrine that in an uncertain world the wise man does best to suspend judgement.

The later sixteenth century has also been called an 'age of criticism'. The term 'critic' was coming into use at the time, in the first place to describe the scholarly editors of classical texts, whose methods of discovering incorrect transcriptions were becoming increasingly sophisticated (the editions by Lipsius of his favourite authors, Tacitus and Seneca, are outstanding examples of this 'textual criticism'). The term gradually widened its meaning to include what we call 'literary criticism' and 'art criticism'. Vasari's *Lives* are among the most famous works of art criticism of the time in which the rival merits of painting and sculpture, colour and drawing, Titian and Michelangelo, were hotly debated in Italy. Treatises were also written to attack or defend Dante, or to lay down the rules for writing epics or tragedies.

All these tendencies, from Platonism to criticism, have their parallels in fifteenth-century Italy, but the changes in emphasis give the later period a character of its own, whether or not we call it the 'age of Mannerism' or (as some scholars have done) the 'autumn' of the Renaissance. Personally, I should prefer to describe the period as one not of 'decline' – the achievement of Michelangelo, Tasso, Montaigne, Shakespeare, Cervantes and others is too stupendous for that – but of 'disintegration' as it was defined at the beginning of this section, a disintegration spread over a long period.

Certain Renaissance elements – favourite attitudes, forms, themes and so on – long survived in European culture. In the reign of pope Urban VIII (1623–44), for example, there was a 'second Roman Renaissance', modelled on the age of pope Leo X, the age of Bembo and Raphael. In France at this time, François de Sales and others have been described with good reason as 'devout humanists', while a certain Nicolas Faret made a success of publishing in 1630 a treatise on 'the art of pleasing at court' which was little more than a translation of sections from Castiglione's *Courtier*. As for England, there is much to be said for describing Robert Burton and Sir Thomas Browne as humanists in the Renaissance sense of that term. Burton's *Anatomy of Melancholy* (1621) opens with a reference to 'Man, the most excellent and noble creature of the world', and quotes endlessly from earlier Renaissance writers such as the philosopher Ficino as well as from Cicero and Seneca. Browne's *Religio Medici* (published 1642 but written in 1635) is a similar meditation on 'the dignity of humanity' as presented in classical texts.

If we include Burton and Browne in the Renaissance, there is obviously a case for Sir William Temple, who defended the superiority of ancient learning and literature over the 'moderns' in an essay written in the 1690s. If we include Temple, it is hard to find good reasons for excluding Jonathan Swift (once Temple's secretary), or indeed Samuel Johnson, Alexander Pope, Edmund Burke and Edward Gibbon, all of whom have been described as leading figures in Augustan 'humanism' [103]. After all, the 'Augustan' age of English culture, the eighteenth century, derives its name from these writers' identification with ancient Roman culture in the time of Augustus. Dr Johnson's poem on London imitates a satire by the Roman writer Juvenal, while Gibbon's *Decline and Fall*, written in the age of the American Revolution, draws an implicit parallel between two declining empires, the Roman and the British. The themes of liberty and corruption, so prominent in the political thought of the eighteenth century, are at once an inheritance from ancient Greece and Rome – via

Renaissance Florence and Venice – and an adaptation of this heritage to the needs of an increasingly commercialised society [104: chs 13–14].

Artists too continued to accept many of the values of the Italian Renaissance. Joshua Reynolds and George Romney both visited Italy to study classical sculpture and Renaissance painting (especially the work of Raphael and Titian). Eighteenth-century English country houses are called 'Palladian' because many of them were inspired by the villa designs of the sixteenth- century Italian architect Andrea Palladio [105]. There was a similar enthusiasm for antiquity in France, in the age of Louis XIV (a ruler who was often compared to Augustus), and again during the French Revolution, when it was the Roman Republic which provided inspiration. In the early nineteenth century, as we have seen, the defenders of the classical tradition in education expressed their identification with Renaissance values by coining the term *Humanismus* [5: ch. 1].

These parallels with the fifteenth and sixteenth centuries are striking ones, and it would not be difficult to add to their number. However, the enthusiasm for antiquity and for Renaissance Italy was gradually changing its meaning as a result of other changes in culture and society. One of the greatest of these changes was the result of the movement historians often call the 'Scientific Revolution' of the seventeenth century, including the work of Galileo Galilei, René Descartes, Isaac Newton and many others. It was nothing less than a new picture of the universe in which the earth was no longer central, the heavens were no longer incorruptible, and the workings of the cosmos could be explained by the laws of mechanics. The investigation of nature was now conducted on the basis of systematic observation and experiment rather than through the study of authoritative ancient texts. Classical and Renaissance views of the universe were now rejected. The new discoveries were considered to demonstrate the superiority of 'moderns' over 'ancients', in some respects at least. The new world-view, as it spread, cut educated men off from the past. It is for such reasons as these that historians date the end or disintegration of the Renaissance to the 1620s and 1630s, the age of Galileo and Descartes [131]. It should now be obvious why it has become impossible to share Burckhardt's view of the Renaissance as obviously 'modern'.

5   Conclusion

In this essay, the Renaissance has been defined rather more narrowly than it was by Burckhardt. It has been considered, following Gombrich's useful distinction, as a 'movement' rather than as a 'period' [13]. Even as a movement, it has been circumscribed fairly tightly, with an emphasis (painting apart) on the attempt to revive antiquity, rather than on the other kinds of cultural change to which Burckhardt and many other historians have drawn attention. These limitations are deliberate. For one thing, a brief essay wich deals with so many branches of learning and the arts and with so many European countries would become intolerably vague if it lacked a sharp focus. Still more important, however, is the fact that almost every other characteristic attributed to the Renaissance can also be found in the Middle Ages, to which it is so often contrasted. Obviously convenient for purposes of exposition, the simple binary opposition between Middle Ages and Renaissance is in many ways seriously misleading.

Take Burckhardt's famous 'development of the individual', for example (a concept about which he admitted having doubts). The notion is not a very clear one. One of its meanings is self-assertiveness, the 'modern sense of fame' as Burckhardt called it. Competitiveness may have been particularly strong in Renaissance Florence – it is impossible to measure it – but as Huizinga pointed out, medieval knights cared a good deal about glory [119]. In their case too fame was the spur.

Another meaning of Renaissance 'individualism' is consciousness of individuality. It is always possible to draw attention, as Burckhardt did in his chapter on 'the discovery of the world and of man', to the rise of biographies and autobiographies in the Italian Renaissance, from the memoirs of pope Pius II to the autobiography of Benvenuto Cellini, and also to the rise of portraits and self-portraits (such as Titian's and Dürer's). Yet autobiographies can also be found – if rather less frequently – in the Middle Ages. For this and other reasons it has been argued that the 'discovery of the individual' came in the twelfth century [120].

Another common way of characterising the Renaissance is in terms of reason; the human reason praised by the humanists, the rational ordering of space made possible by the discovery of perspective, or what Burckhardt called 'the spirit of calculation', illustrating it from the statistics collected by the Venetian Republic in the fifteenth century. Here too the division between Renaissance and Middle Ages has come to seem an artificial one. The scholastic philosophers had a positive attitude to reason: perhaps they should be described as 'scholastic humanists'. An interest in precise figures can be found in western Europe in the twelfth century if not before. It was encouraged by the growing employment of two kinds of calculating-machine, the abacus (which was in use in the eleventh century) and the mechanical clock (in use in the fourteenth). In other words, numeracy was not new in the age of Bruni and Brunelleschi [122, 127]. Indeed, it has become difficult to argue that there was any fundamental change in the psychology or mentality of even an educated minority between the Middle Ages and the Renaissance (whether this transition is placed around 1500, 1400 or 1300). At this point it may be worth pausing to take stock and to enquire whether the Renaissance may not be in danger of dissolving altogether, for two rather different kinds of reason.

In the first place, it was defined by Burckhardt as the beginning of modernity, a concept about which historians have become increasingly unhappy since his day, partly because it implies a simple evolutionary model of cultural change which many of us now reject, and partly because in the last generation or so, westerners have come to think, more or less uneasily, that what they are living in is actually a 'post-modern' world. For anyone who holds such views, the Renaissance will now seem rather more remote than it did [132].

In the second place, although the achievements of Petrarch, Leonardo and so many other artists, writers and scholars still compel admiration, it has become much harder than it was in Burckhardt's day to separate their achievements from those of the Middle Ages on one side and from those of the seventeenth and eighteenth centuries on the other. Aristotle, to take an ob-

58

vious example, was the master of many European intellectuals from his rediscovery in the thirteenth century to his rejection some four hundred years later, and the humanist debates about his philosophy are easier to understand if they are considered in the perspective of this longer period. Again, historians of the Middle Ages object to the restriction of the term 'humanist' to scholars and thinkers from Petrarch onwards on the grounds that the idea of the 'dignity of man' was current in the twelfth and thirteenth centuries [127].

Where does this leave us? There is no consensus. Some scholars in the field of what is still called 'Renaissance studies' go on as if nothing had happened. Others, including the present author, are trying to relocate what happened in fourteenth-century Florence, fifteenth-century Italy and sixteenth-century Europe in a sequence of connected changes between 1000 (or thereabouts) and 1800. These long-term developments might be described as the 'westernisation of the west' in the sense that they made upper-class Europeans, at least, increasingly different from other peoples, as the history of the 'discovery' and conquest of much of the globe was to reveal. Some of these developments were technological: the invention of firearms, mechanical clocks, printing, new kinds of sailing-ship and of machines which speeded up spinning and weaving. The changes which will be emphasised here, however, are changes in mentality, two in particular.

In an important study, the sociologist Norbert Elias argued that the sixteenth century was a crucial period in the west for what he called the 'civilising process', in other words the development of self-control; quoting among other evidence the treatises on good manners by Erasmus and by the Italian bishop Giovanni Della Casa, both of them frequently reprinted in a number of languages [128]. There seems little doubt that concern for civilised behaviour at table (refraining from spitting, washing one's hands before meals, and so on) was widely shared at that time, at least in certain social circles, but (as Elias admits) it is impossible to draw a sharp line between Renaissance and Middle Ages. Medieval books on 'courtesy' go back as far as the tenth century [123].

It should be emphasised that no one is suggesting that all other cultures (traditional Japan, for instance, or China) lacked a sense of restraint at table and elsewhere. Western courtesy or civilisation was one set of conventions among others. It might therefore be more exact to talk of the rise of a sense of privacy, or of a gradual change in assumptions about the relative spheres of public and private life, as the upper classes began to eat from individual plates rather than from communal dishes, to sit on individual chairs rather than communal benches, and to think it ill-mannered to offer a guest (to quote Della Casa's example) 'fruit from which you have already taken a bite'. These changes may well have something to do with Burckhardt's 'individualism', but they were spread thinly over a much longer period than the Renaissance. They are perhaps associated with other forms of restraint or repression, notably the sexual repression which seems to have become a characteristic of western culture in this period.

A second approach to cultural changes in the medieval and early modern periods stresses the effect on mentalities of changes in the modes of communication. Historians of rhetoric have noted the increasing concern with the art of persuasion, whether by public speeches or private letters, revealed by the treatises on the subject produced in Italy in particular from the time of the Benedictine monk Alberic of Monte Cassino, at the end of the eleventh century [124]. Some of them would go so far as to speak of a 'rhetorical revolution' or even a 'language revolution' in the later Middle Ages, pointing out that philosophers were becoming conscious that the relation between language and reality was problematic. Rhetoric is a discipline concerned with gestures as well as words, and its study seems to have encouraged the sense of social role, the concern with the presentation of self so evident in Castiglione's *Courtier* or in the lives of men as different as Thomas More and Walter Raleigh [81, 106].

Others have stressed the spread of literacy in the Middle Ages, for both commercial and administrative reasons. The self- consciousness which fascinated Burckhardt may have been one of the consequences of the new habit of solitary reading and writing [125]. Yet other historians place the emphasis on what they call 'print culture'. It is not always easy to distinguish between the consequences of printing and those of an earlier rise of literacy and numeracy, but at least it can be said that in the long run the invention of printing increased the availability of information, thus widening mental horizons and encouraging critical attitudes to authority by making the discrepancies between different authors more visible [133].

Why this particular cluster of changes should have taken place in the fifteenth and sixteenth centuries is – like most fundamental questions in history – difficult to grasp, but it is at least possible to offer a few hypotheses. The concern with rhetoric developed in the city-states of Italy where the involvement of the citizens in government made the art of persuasion particularly necessary [67: ch. 2]. The growth of international trade (in which Italy once again played a central role) encouraged literacy because of the need to record commercial transactions and to keep accounts. The development of increasingly centralised states also encouraged the use of written records and so increased the need for literacy. Norbert Elias has even suggested that the civilising process is ultimately connected with political centralisation. People are forced by the central power to live at peace with one another and more gradually to exercise restraint in other ways as well. The increasing concern with military discipline (including drill) in the sixteenth century is one argument in favour of this hypothesis, and the neostoic movement, discussed earlier, demonstrates the link between the cult of self-control and the growing interest in particular ancient writers, Seneca in particular [70]. For the later classical world had also been centralised, and many of the 'new' problems which arose between the eleventh and eighteenth centuries had once been 'ancient' ones. A debate over civilisation, or courtesy, for example, had already taken place (in terms of *urbanitas* or 'urbanity') in the Rome of Cicero.

As these examples suggest, the appeal of the classics in the whole period, and in the fifteenth and sixteenth centuries in particular, was largely the result of their practical relevance. The ancients were admired because they were guides to living. Following them meant travelling with more security in the direction in which people were already going.

Select Bibliography

This bibliography, expanded for the second edition, remains confined to works available in English. Unless otherwise mentioned, the place of publication is London.

For the most recent work in Renaissance studies, see specialist journals such as *Renaissance Studies, Renaissance Quarterly, Bibliothèque d'humanisme et renaissance* (which includes articles in English), and the *Journal of the Warburg and Courtauld Institutes*.

Introductions

[1] J. Burckhardt, *The Civilisation of the Renaissance in Italy* (first published in German in 1860; English trans. 1878, repr. Harmondsworth, 1990), remains indispensable, although many of the conclusions have been challenged.

[2] D. Hay, *The Italian Renaissance in its Historical Background* (second edn, Cambridge, 1977). A balanced survey.

[3] E. H. Gombrich, *The Story of Art* (14th edn, 1984), chs 12–18.

[4] E. Panofsky, *Renaissance and Renascences in Western Art* (1970). This lucid and elegant essay places the Renaissance in the long history of classical revivals.

[5] P. O. Kristeller, *Renaissance Thought* (New York, 1961). A classic account.

[6] P. Burke, *Culture and Society in Renaissance Italy* (1972; revised edn, *The Italian Renaissance*, Cambridge, 1987). Attempts to place the arts in their social context.

[7] L. Martines, *Power and Imagination: City-States in Renaissance Italy* (1980). Crude but vigorous and especially useful on continuities between the twelfth and thirteenth centuries and the Renaissance.

[8] J. R. Hale (ed.), *A Concise Encyclopedia of the Italian Renaissance* (1981). A useful work of reference.

[9] E. Garin (ed.), *Renaissance Characters* (1988). Essays on the prince, the merchant, the courtier, the lady, etc.

[10] J. R. Hale, *The Civilization of the Renaissance in Europe* (1993). Characteristically lively and wide-ranging.

The Idea of the Renaissance

[11] J. Huizinga, 'The Problem of the Renaissance' (1920), repr. in his *Men and Ideas* (1960). The reflections of a great cultural historian.

[12] W. K. Ferguson, *The Renaissance in Historical Thought* (Cambridge, Mass., 1948). The history of the idea from the humanists to the mid-twentieth century.

[13] E. H. Gombrich, 'The Renaissance – Period or Movement?', in *Background to the English Renaissance*, ed. J. B. Trapp (1974).

[14] J. B. Bullen, *The Myth of the Renaissance in Nineteenth-Century Writing* (Oxford, 1994). Concentrates on England and France.

[15] W. Kerrigan and G. Braden, *The Idea of the Renaissance* (Baltimore, 1989). Focuses on Burckhardt and Cassirer.

Original Texts

[16] L. Bruni, 'Panegyric to the City of Florence', trans. in *The Earthly Republic*, ed. B. J. Kohl and R. G. Witt (Philadelphia, 1978), pp. 135–75.

[17] G. Pico, 'Oration on the Dignity of Man', trans. in *The Renaissance Philosophy of Man*, ed. E. Cassirer *et al.* (Chicago, 1948), pp. 223–54.

[18] N. Machiavelli, *The Prince*, trans. ed. Q. Skinner and R. Price (Cambridge, 1988).

[19] B. Castiglione, *The Courtier*, trans. G. Bull (revised edn, Harmondsworth, 1976).

[20] G. Vasari, *Lives of the Artists*, selections trans. G. Bull (2 vols, Harmondsworth, 1965, 1987).

[21] Erasmus, *Ciceronianus*, in *Collected Works*, vol. 28 (Toronto, 1986).
[22] M. de Montaigne, *Essays*, trans. M. Screech (1993).

Italy: Painting and Graphics

[23] E. Panofsky, *Studies in Iconology* (New York, 1939). The most celebrated example of the 'iconographical' approach to meaning in the visual arts.
[24] E. Wind, *Pagan Mysteries in the Renaissance* (revised edn, Oxford, 1980). Learned and ingenious neoplatonic interpretations of Botticelli, Titian, etc.
[25] E. H. Gombrich, *Symbolic Images* (1972). A more sceptical approach to the same cluster of problems.
[26] M. Baxandall, *Painting and Experience in Fifteenth-Century Italy* (Oxford, 1972). A historical anthropology of visual communication.
[27] C. Hope, 'Artists, patrons and advisers in the Italian Renaissance', in *Patronage in the Renaissance*, ed. G. F. Lytle and S. Orgel (Princeton, 1981). A critique of the recent emphasis on learned programmes for paintings.
[28] B. Cole, *The Renaissance Artist at Work* (1983). Deals with training, raw materials and genres.
[29] S. Edgerton, *The Renaissance Rediscovery of Linear Perspective* (New York, 1975).
[30] B. Kempers, *Painting, Power and Patronage: The Rise of the Professional Artist in Renaissance Italy* (English trans. London, 1992). Emphasises links between state formation, civilisation and professionalisation.
[31] J. Pope-Hennessy, *The Portrait in the Renaissance* (1966).
[32] D. Landau and P. Parshall, *The Renaissance Print 1470–1550* (New Haven, 1994).

Italy: Sculpture and Architecture

[33] C. Avery, *Florentine Renaissance Sculpture* (1970). A brief introduction.
[34] C. Seymour, *Sculpture in Italy, 1400–1500* (Harmondsworth, 1970). A full survey.

[35] R. Wittkower, *Architectural Principles in the Age of Humanism* (1949). Does for architecture what Panofsky did for painting.
[36] P. Murray, *The Architecture of the Italian Renaissance* (1963). A lucid and businesslike introduction.
[37] L. Heydenreich and W. Lotz, *Architecture in Italy, 1400–1600* (Harmondsworth, 1974). A thorough scrutiny.
[38] J. Ackerman, *The Villa: Form and Ideology of Country Houses* (1990).
[39] D. Howard, *The Architectural History of Venice* (1980).
[40] P. Thornton, *The Italian Renaissance Interior* (1991).
[41] C. Lazzaro, *The Italian Renaissance Garden* (New Haven, 1990).

Italy: Intellectual History

[42] E. Garin, *Italian Humanism* (1947; English trans. Oxford, 1965). Frequently criticised but not superseded.
[43] H. Baron, *The Crisis of the Early Italian Renaissance* (Princeton, 1955). Stresses the links between republican politics and 'civic humanism'.
[44] J. Seigel, 'Civic Humanism or Ciceronian Rhetoric?', *Past and Present*, 34 (1966). A critique of Baron, to which he replied in the same journal.
[45] A. Grafton and L. Jardine, *From Humanism to the Humanities* (1986). A critique of Garin, placing more stress on practice, the social context and women.
[46] P. Grendler, *Schooling in Renaissance Italy* (Baltimore, 1989).
[47] P. Burke, *The Renaissance Sense of the Past* (1969). An anthology of texts with commentaries designed to illustrate the rise of a sense of cultural distance from the past.
[48] F. Gilbert, *Machiavelli and Guicciardini* (Princeton, 1965). A penetrating study of two major figures on the edge of humanism.
[49] C. L. Stinger, *Humanism and the Church Fathers* (Albany, 1977).
[50] F. Yates, *Giordano Bruno and the Hermetic Tradition* (1964). Stresses humanist interest in the occult.
[51] E. Garin, *Astrology in the Renaissance* (1983).
[52] C. Schmitt and Q. Skinner, (eds) *The Cambridge History of Renaissance Philosophy* (Cambridge, 1988).

66

[53] B. P. Copenhaver and C. Schmitt, *Renaissance Philosophy* (Oxford, 1992).

Renaissance outside Italy: Visual Arts

[54] E. Rosenthal, 'The Diffusion of the Italian Renaissance Style in Western Europe', *Sixteenth-Century Journal* 9 (1978).

[55] A. Blunt, *Art and Architecture in France* (4th edn, Harmondsworth, 1980).

[56] M. Baxandall, *The Limewood Sculptors of Renaissance Germany* (1980). Of much wider interest than the title suggests.

[57] J. Bialostocki, *Art of the Renaissance in Eastern Europe* (1976). A fine study of the 'reception' of Italian forms.

[58] R. J. Knecht, *Renaissance Warrior and Patron: Francis I* (2nd edn, Cambridge, 1994).

[59] T. D. Kaufmann, *Court, Cloister and City* (Princeton, 1995).

[60] J. Chipps Smith, *German Sculpture of the Later Renaissance, c.1520–80: Art in an Age of Uncertainty* (Princeton, 1994).

[61] M. Howard, 'Self-Fashioning and the Classical Moment in Mid-Sixteenth-Century English Architecture', in L. Gent and N. Llewellyn (eds) *Renaissance Bodies* (1990).

[62] M. Howard and N. Llewellyn, 'Painting and Images', in *The Cambridge Cultural History of Britain*, vol. 3, ed. B. Ford (1989).

[63] L. Campbell, *Renaissance Portraits* (1990).

Renaissance outside Italy: Ideas

[64] D. P. Walker, *The Ancient Theology* (1972). On attempts to reconcile neoplatonism with Christianity.

[65] F. Yates, *Astraea* (1972). Important essays on the political meanings of festivals, poetry, painting etc. in England and France.

[66] D. Kelley, *Foundations of Modern Historical Scholarship* (New York, 1970). French humanists on the relation between language, law and history.

[67] Q. Skinner, *Foundations of Modern Political Thought* (2 vols, Cambridge, 1978).

[68] J. Bentley, *Humanists and Holy Writ* (Princeton, 1983).

[69] G. Kipling, *The Triumph of Honour: Burgundian Origins of the Elizabethan Renaissance* (Leiden, 1977).

[70] G. Oestreich, *Neostoicism and the Early Modern State* (Cambridge, 1982). Especially concerned with the Netherlands and with Justus Lipsius.

[71] A. Goodman and A. McKay (eds), *The Impact of Humanism on Western Europe* (1990).

[72] R. Porter and M. Teich (eds), *The Renaissance in National Context* (Cambridge, 1992). Especially strong on Central and Eastern Europe.

[73] C. Nauert, *Humanism and the Culture of Renaissance Europe* (Cambridge, 1995). A lucid and balanced survey.

Literature

[74] A. J. Krailsheimer (ed.), *The Continental Renaissance* (Harmondsworth, 1971). Introductory survey of France, Germany, Italy and Spain.

[75] L. Forster, *The Icy Fire* (Cambridge, 1969). A comparative study of Petrarchism.

[76] M. Bakhtin, *Rabelais and his World* (1965; English trans., Cambridge, Mass., 1968). On the relation between popular culture and one of the masterpieces of Renaissance literature.

[77] T. Cave, *The Cornucopian Text* (Oxford, 1979). On awareness of the problems of writing in Erasmus, Rabelais, Ronsard and Montaigne.

[78] T. Greene, *The Light in Troy* (1982). On imitation and assimilation in Italian, French and Engish poetry.

[79] D. Javitch, *Poetry and Courtliness in Renaissance England* (Princeton, 1978). On Sidney, Spenser, etc.

[80] S. Orgel, *The Illusion of Power* (Berkeley and Los Angeles, 1975). On theatre and politics in the English Renaissance.

[81] S. Greenblatt, *Renaissance Self-Fashioning from More to Shakespeare* (1980). A fresh look at Renaissance individualism.

[82] S. Greenblatt, *Shakespearian Negotiations: The Circulation of Social Energy in Renaissance England* (Oxford, 1988). Approaches Shakespeare via studies of exorcism, hermaphrodites, etc.

[83] F. Rico, *The Spanish Picaresque Novel and the Point of View* (1969; English trans., Cambridge, 1984).

[84] P. Fumerton, *Cultural Aesthetics: Renaissance Literature and the Practice of Social Ornament* (Chicago, 1991). On connections between the arts in Elizabethan England.

[85] D. Quint, *Epic and Empire* (Princeton, 1993). On links between poetry and politics.

[86] P. Burke, *The Fortunes of the Courtier* (1995). The history of translations and adaptations of, and responses to, Castiglione's famous dialogue.

Music, Mathematics and Science

[87] C. Palisca, *Humanism in Italian Renaissance Musical Thought* (New Haven, 1985). A full survey.

[88] E. E. Lowinsky, 'Music in the Culture of the Renaissance', *Journal of the History of Ideas*, 15 (1954), rpr. in *Renaissance Essays*, ed. P. O. Kristeller and P. P. Wiener (New York, 1968), ch. 14.

[89] G. Tomlinson, *Music in Renaissance Magic* (Chicago, 1993).

[90] J. A. Owens, 'Was There a Renaissance in Music?', in *Language and Images of Renaissance Italy*, ed. A. Brown (1995), ch. 4.

[91] P. L. Rose, *The Italian Renaissance of Mathematics* (Geneva, 1975).

[92] A. Debus, *Man and Nature in the Renaissance* (Cambridge, 1978). General survey, particularly useful on alchemy.

[93] M. B. Hall, 'Problems of the Scientific Renaissance', in D. Hay *et al.*, *The Renaissance* (1982).

Women in the Renaissance

[94] M. King, *Women of the Renaissance* (1991). A general survey.

[95] C. Jordan, *Renaissance Feminism* (Ithaca, 1990). A close analysis of texts.

[96] I. Maclean, *The Renaissance Notion of Woman* (Cambridge, 1980). Compares legal, medical and other discourses.

[97] J. Kelly, 'Did Women Have a Renaissance?', in her *Women, History and Theory* (Chicago, 1984), ch. 2.

[98] P. Benson, *The Invention of the Renaissance Woman* (Philadelphia, 1992).

The Disintegration of the Renaissance

[99] J. Shearman, *Mannerism* (Harmondsworth, 1967). A lively survey of all the arts.

[100] A. Chastel, *The Sack of Rome* (Princeton, 1983). On the cultural consequences of the catastrophe of 1527.

[101] R. J. W. Evans, *Rudolf II and his World* (Oxford, 1973). Discusses humanism and Mannerism.

[102] R. R. Bolgar (ed.), *Classical Influences in European Culture, 1500–1700* (Cambridge, 1976). Follows the fortunes of the classical tradition.

[103] P. Fussell, *The Rhetorical World of Augustan Humanism* (Oxford, 1965). Presents Swift, Pope, Johnson, Reynolds, Gibbon and Burke as late Renaissance humanists.

[104] J. G. A. Pocock, *The Machiavellian Moment* (Princeton, 1975). Includes an important discussion of civic humanism in Anglo-American thought in the seventeenth and eighteenth centuries.

[105] R. Wittkower, *Palladio and English Palladianism* (1974).

Individuals

[106] R. W. Hanning and D. Rosand (eds), *Castiglione: the Ideal and the Real in Renaissance Culture* (1983).

[107] P. Russell, *Cervantes* (1985).

[108] E. Panofsky, *Albrecht Dürer* (4th edn, Princeton, 1955).

[109] J. McConica, *Erasmus* (1986).

[110] M. Kemp, *Leonardo da Vinci* (1981).

[111] Q. Skinner, *Machiavelli* (1980).

[112] H. Hibbard, *Michelangelo* (1975).

[113] P. Burke, *Montaigne* (1981).

[114] A. Fox, *Thomas More: History and Providence* (1982).

[115] N. Mann, *Petrarch* (1985).

[116] W. G. Craven, *Giovanni Pico della Mirandola* (Geneva, 1981).

[117] M. M. Screech, *Rabelais* (1979).

[118] R. Jones and N. Penny, *Raphael* (1983).

Middle Ages

[119] J. Huizinga, *The Waning of the Middle Ages* (1919; complete English trans., Chicago, 1995). The equivalent for France and Flanders of Burckhardt on Italy.

[120] C. Morris, *The Discovery of the Individual: 1050–1200* (1972).

[121] C. Brooke, *The Twelfth-Century Renaissance* (1969).

[122] A. Murray, *Reason and Society in the Middle Ages* (Oxford, 1978). A major study in the history of mentalities.

[123] C. S. Jaeger, *The Origins of Courtliness* (Philadelphia, 1985). Stresses the role of German bishops in the High Middle Ages.

[124] J. J. Murphy, *Rhetoric in the Middle Ages* (Berkeley, 1974).

[125] H. J. Chaytor, *From Script to Print* (Cambridge, 1945).

[126] R. R. Bolgar (ed.), *Classical Influences on European Culture 500–1500* (Cambridge, 1971).

[127] R. W. Southern, *Scholastic Humanism and the Unification of Europe* (Oxford, 1995).

Wider perspectives

[128] N. Elias, *The History of Manners* (1939; English trans., Oxford, 1978). The historical sociology of everyday life.

[129] A. Toynbee, *A Study of History*, vol. 9 (Oxford, 1954).

[130] L. D. Reynolds and N. G. Wilson, *Scribes and Scholars* (2nd edn, Oxford, 1974). On the transmission, recovery and criticism of the manuscripts of classical texts.

[131] C. Schmitt, 'Towards a Reassessment of Renaissance Aristotelianism', *History of Science*, vol. 11 (1973). Emphasises the survival of this system of ideas into the seventeenth century.

[132] W. Bouwsma, 'The Renaissance and the Drama of European History', repr. in his *Usable Past* (Berkeley, 1990), ch. 16.

[133] E. Eisenstein, *The Printing Revolution* (Cambridge, 1983). Emphasises the role of the press in cultural and social change.

Index

75